CW01313958

FROM
TEE
TO
GREEN

TIPS AND TRICKS FOR
TODAY'S GOLFER

DRIVER
3 WOOD
5 WOOD

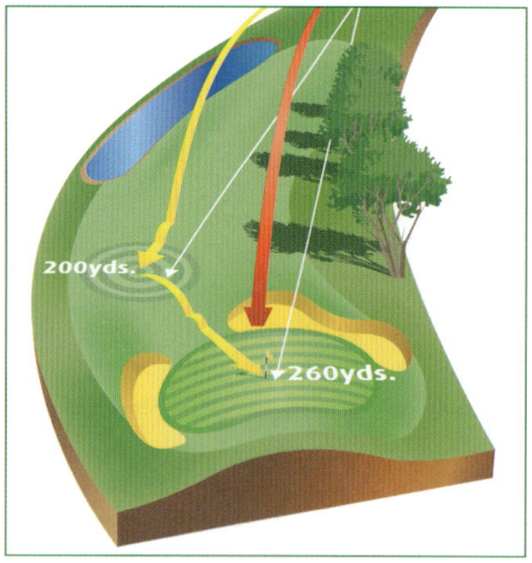
200yds.
260yds.

SW
PW
9 IRON
8 IRON
7 IRON
6 IRON

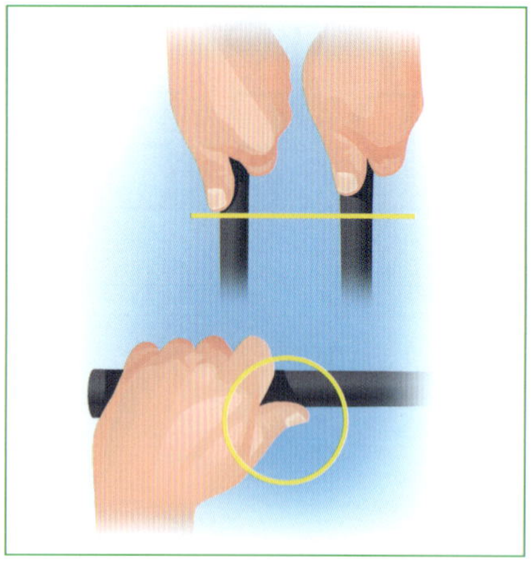

FROM TEE TO GREEN

TIPS AND TRICKS FOR TODAY'S GOLFER

Today's Golfer MAGAZINE

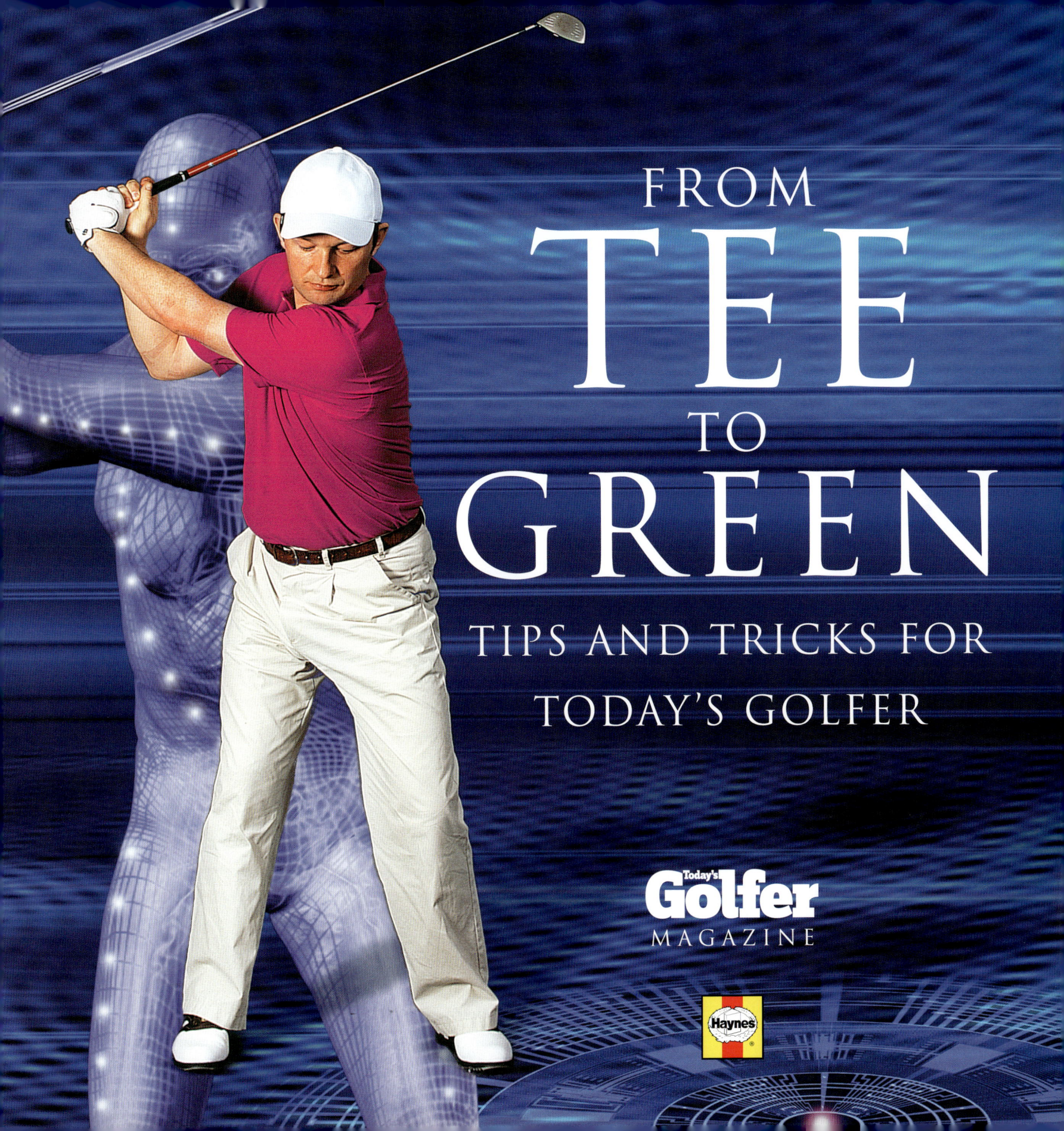

Haynes

Materials © Emap Active Limited 2007
Compilation and cover design © Haynes Publishing 2007

All rights reserved. No part of this publication may be reproduced, stored in a retrieval system or transmitted, in any form or by any means, electronic, mechanical, photocopying, recording or otherwise, without prior permission in writing from the publisher.

First published in 2007

A catalogue record for this book is available from the British Library

ISBN 978 1 84425 429 3

Published jointly by
Haynes Publishing, Sparkford,
Yeovil, Somerset BA22 7JJ, England
Phone 01963 440635, www.haynes.co.uk
and
Emap Active Limited,
Wentworth House, Wentworth Street,
Peterborough PE1 1DS, England
Phone 01733 213700, www.emap.com

Book Editorial Director, Scott Mauck
Book Publications Director, Jeremy Yates-Round
Book Design and Production, Eileen Fore and Kent Reppert

Printed and bound in England by J.H. Haynes & Co. Ltd, Sparkford

CONTENTS

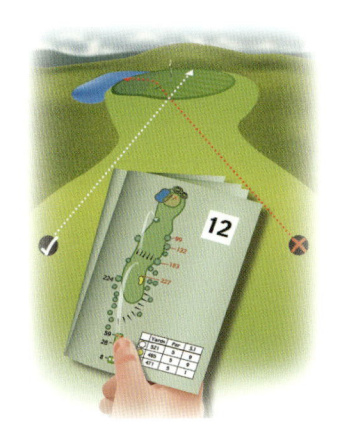

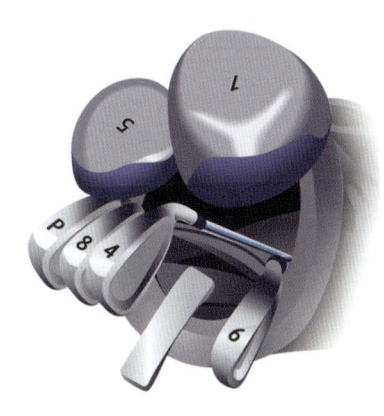

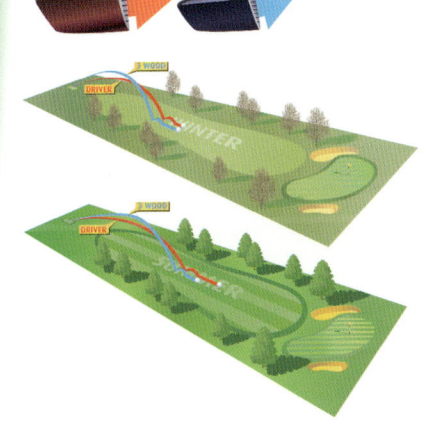

FOREWORD BY ANDY CALTON 7

Fundamentals
EQUIPMENT 9
THE GRIP 13
THE SET-UP 20
THE SWING 32
MENTAL GAME 46
SHOT-MAKING 54
WEIGHT TRANSFER 56
FAULT-FIXING 57
CONSISTENT PLAY 60
COMPETITION 62
HIT IT FURTHER 64

Practice
THE SWING 66
COURSE MANAGEMENT 69
FUNDAMENTALS 74

From the tee 79

Around the green 84
PRACTICE TIPS 94

On the green 106
PRACTICE TIPS 116

In the bunker 122

Trouble shots 128

Fault-fixing 138

Course management 144

6

Foreword
by Andy Calton

Today's Golfer has always tried to help people play better. Every month the magazine carries loads of drills, tips and lessons . . . but rarely do you get the whole game covered extensively in one place. That's what this book is all about.

Here, some of the best teaching professionals in the UK share their wisdom to help you get the ball from the tee and into the hole in as few shots as possible. From smashing one off the tee, to those touchy short shots around the green.. we cover the lot.

Every tip, drill and lesson has been compiled by TG's experts. This book should help you and hopefully it will inspire you. Playing better is not just about striking the ball better. It's about feeling good about the game. About wanting to try something out so badly, you can't wait for your next game. About chipping in the garden, about putting on the carpet, about practising your swing by the coffee machine.

If this book helps you get better and helps you want to get better, it will have done its job. Good luck!

Andy Calton

The publisher would like to acknowledge the diligent efforts of Susan Voss and the staff of Emap Licensing for making this project possible.

Fundamentals INTRODUCTION

The Grip

The Right Equipment

The Set-up

The Swing

The Mental Game

EQUIPMENT

Too thick »

Too thin »

EQUIPMENT CHECK
Handy advice on grip thickness

Grips that are too thick automatically restrict the necessary speedy hand action to release the clubhead fully through the hitting zone and prevent the clubface returning to square at impact.

Conversely, grips that are too thin usually promote over-active hands, causing the clubface to close through impact and result in the ball being drawn or pulled to the left.

A perfect fit is when the fingernails of the top hand on the club just touch the fleshy pad at the base of the hand. The grips are too thick if the tips of the fingers fail to reach the palm and too thin if the fingers dig into your palms.

Correct »

Fundamentals EQUIPMENT

CHOOSING EQUIPMENT

Give them a sporting chance

It's a great disappointment how many youngsters give up the game after only a few outings because they find it too difficult.

Unfortunately, their problems often arise because they try to play with clubs just not suited to their build – often handed down by their parents or grandparents.

Clubs that are too long and heavy make it virtually impossible to stand correctly at address and result in all sorts of problems, the main one being hitting the ball out of the neck of the clubhead.

Any youngster keen on playing the game should give themselves a sporting chance of success by seeking advice on equipment from a PGA-qualified professional.

Clubs that are too long will cause bad posture and strikes from out of the neck of the club.

This is how you should look at address for good ball-striking.

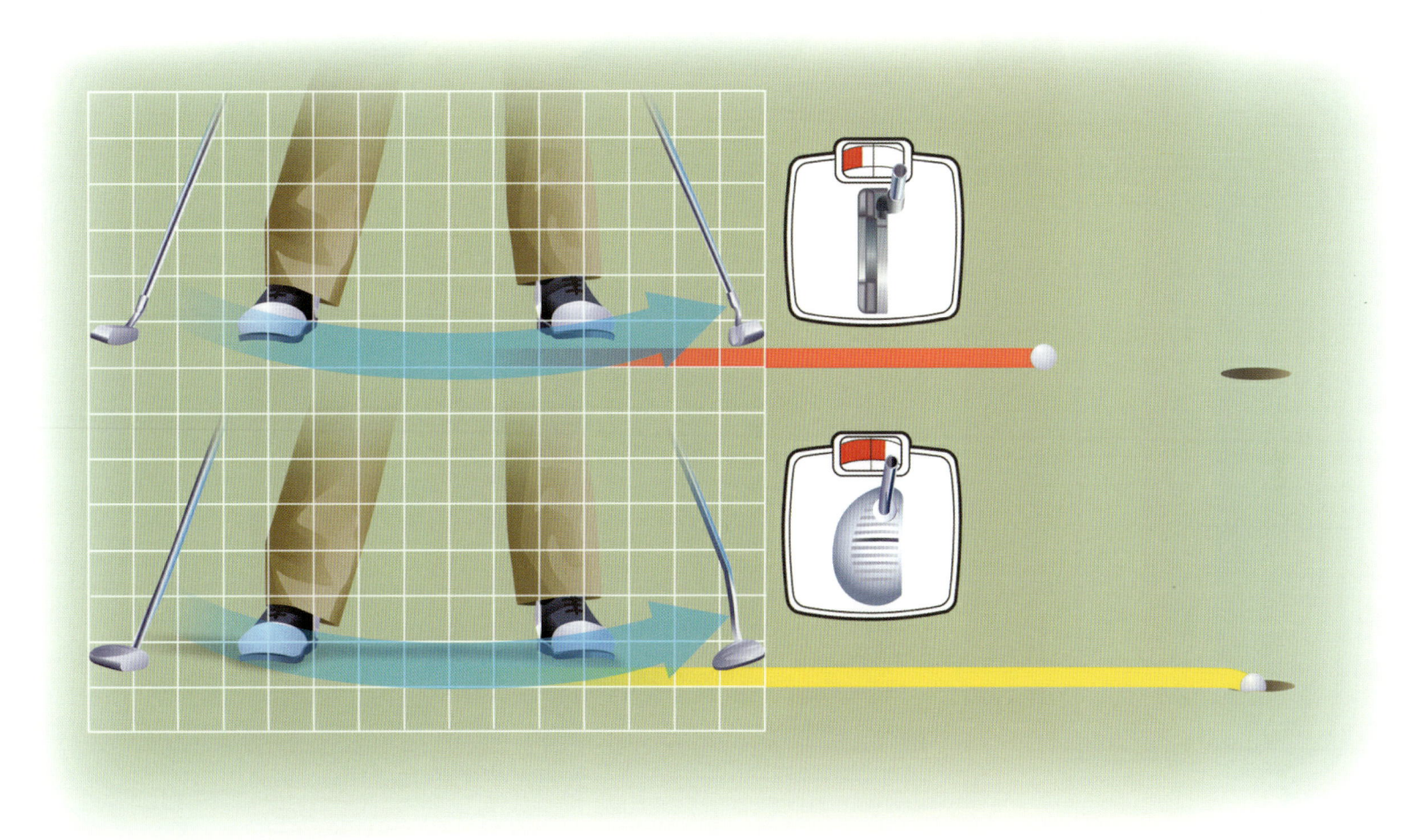

WINTER PUTTING

A stroke for all seasons

Are you one of the many players who have difficulty adapting their putting stroke to suit the slower greens during the wet winter months? Well, here's some good news...you don't have to.

By simply using a heavier putter, you can retain exactly the same stroke that impressed all those who played with you during the summer!

And if you just can't bear the thought of parting company with your favourite putter during the winter months, lead tape can be added to the head to increase the weight. But it's easy to mess up the balance, so it's best to let your local PGA pro do the job for you.

Fundamentals EQUIPMENT

SHAFT TECHNOLOGY

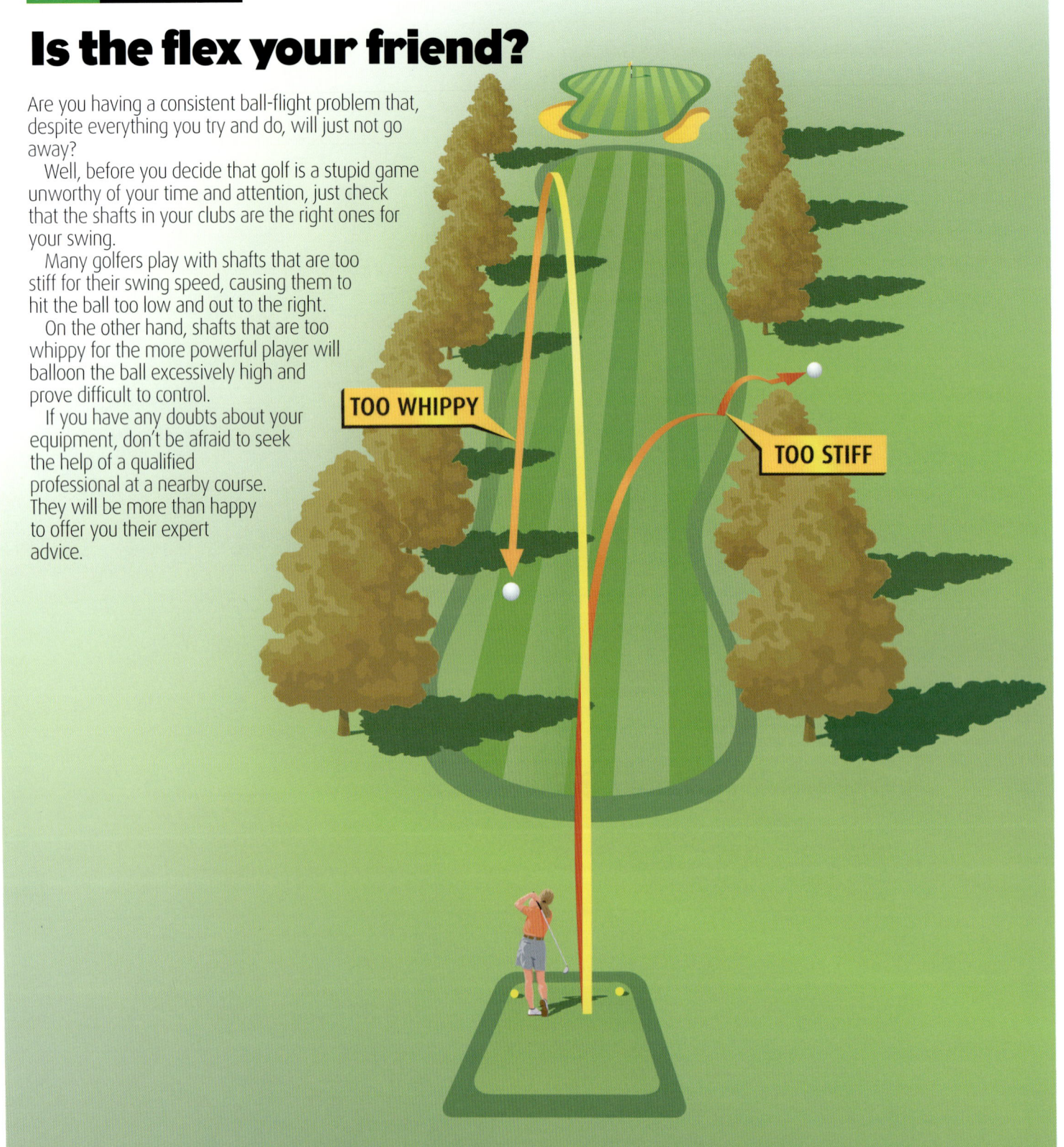

Is the flex your friend?

Are you having a consistent ball-flight problem that, despite everything you try and do, will just not go away?

Well, before you decide that golf is a stupid game unworthy of your time and attention, just check that the shafts in your clubs are the right ones for your swing.

Many golfers play with shafts that are too stiff for their swing speed, causing them to hit the ball too low and out to the right.

On the other hand, shafts that are too whippy for the more powerful player will balloon the ball excessively high and prove difficult to control.

If you have any doubts about your equipment, don't be afraid to seek the help of a qualified professional at a nearby course. They will be more than happy to offer you their expert advice.

TOO WHIPPY

TOO STIFF

THE GRIP

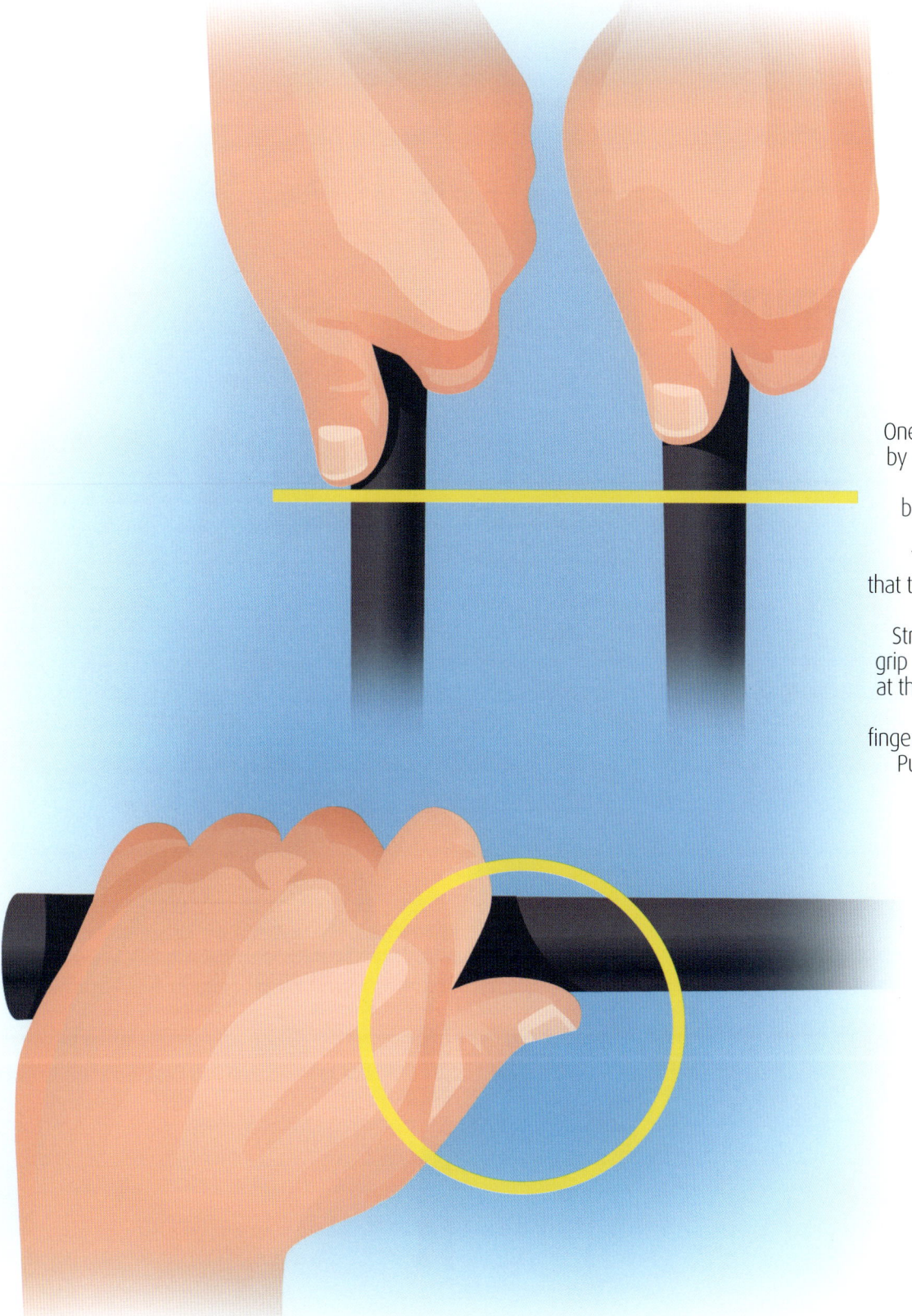

OVER-SWINGING

Long and short of it

One of the most common faults committed by golfers is over-swinging, where the club travels beyond parallel at the top of the backswing – leading to loss of control and therefore poor distance and accuracy. Yet very few of them realise, or are told, that the cause could lie in the way they place their left thumb on the club at address. Stretching the left thumb too far down the grip offers very little support to the clubhead at the top and is often seen with youngsters who use a baseball grip (where all the fingers of the lower hand are on the handle). Pulling it up so there is no gap between it and the forefinger places the hands in a much stronger position to bear the weight of the shaft.

Fundamentals THE GRIP

LIGHT TOUCH
Pressure point

Ask any experienced golf teacher for his list of the most common mistakes made by club golfers and you can safely bet a few quid that gripping the club too tightly will feature prominently.

'Tee to Green' has often attempted to put a fix on the exact degree of pressure that should be applied…using tubes of toothpaste, birds in hands and scales of one to ten to illustrate the point.

And here's another: take your normal grip and hold the club in front of you so that the shaft is vertical. Now relax the hands very slowly until you feel the club begin to slip through your fingers. The ideal grip pressure should be a tad firmer than the moment before the club starts to slip.

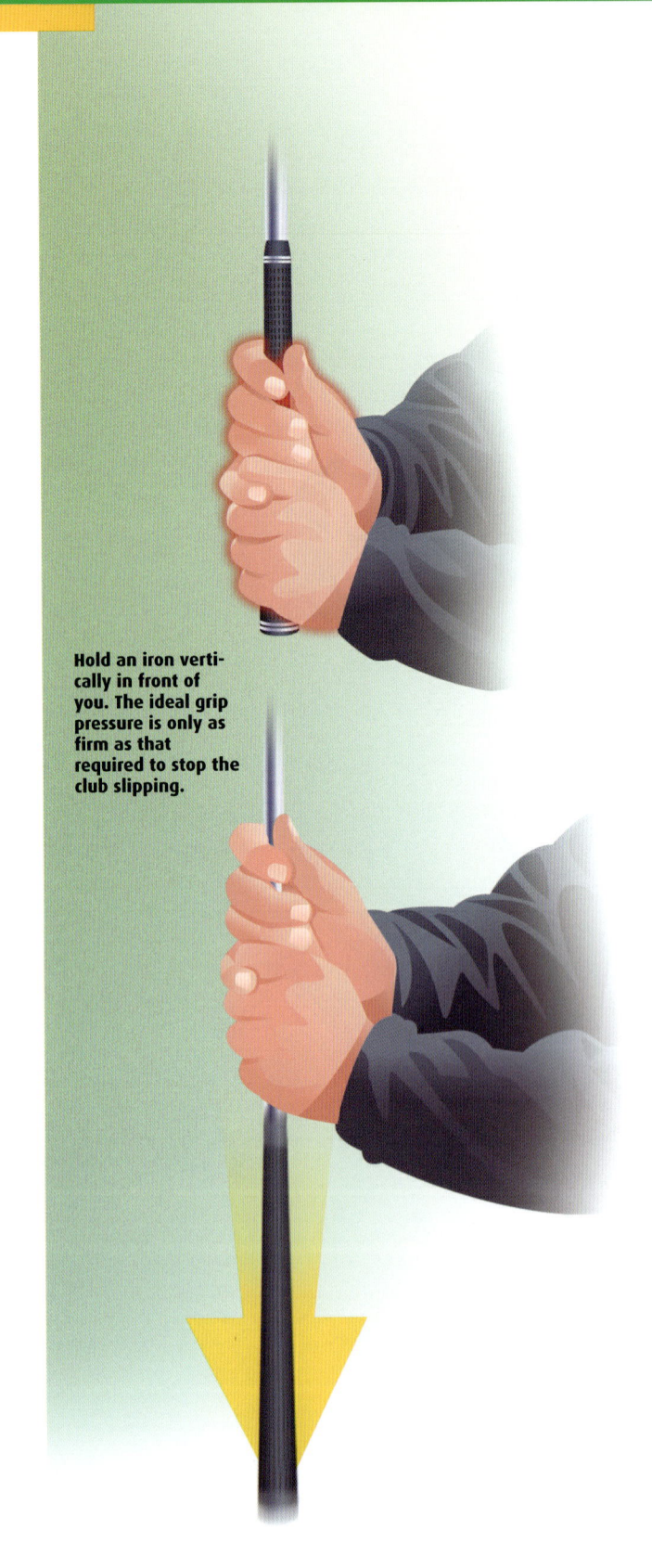

Hold an iron vertically in front of you. The ideal grip pressure is only as firm as that required to stop the club slipping.

LIGHT TOUCH

Take it easy

Watch David Beckham taking a free kick or a top tennis star like Pete Sampras hitting an outright winner and you can't help but notice the complete lack of tension in their bodies. Just the same applies to all the top Tour professionals when they fizz the ball off the tee.

If only the same could be said of the average club golfer! The vast majority give themselves no chance of achieving a smooth, fluid swing by gripping the club as though they were strangling a snake and tensing their muscles until they are almost bursting.

Here are three simple tips to help reduce what all teachers agree is the biggest swing-killer in the game.

1 Grip the club firmly but lightly. On a scale of one *(lightest)* to ten *(tightest)*, the pressure should be four or five.

2 Make sure your chin is off your chest (ie not pressed tightly into it) and all your muscles are relaxed.

3 Waggle the club lightly back and forth before starting your swing.

Fundamentals THE GRIP

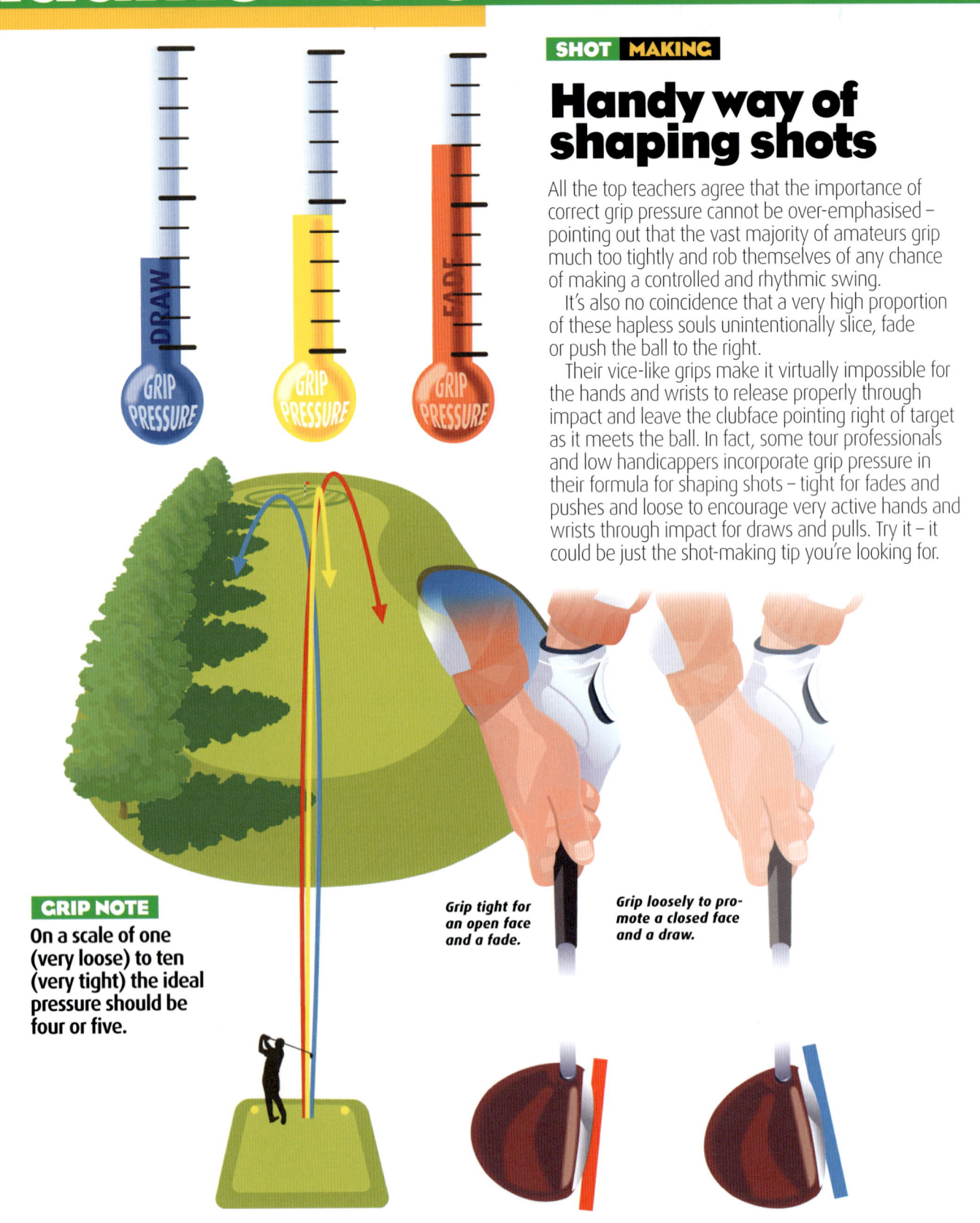

SHOT MAKING

Handy way of shaping shots

All the top teachers agree that the importance of correct grip pressure cannot be over-emphasised – pointing out that the vast majority of amateurs grip much too tightly and rob themselves of any chance of making a controlled and rhythmic swing.

It's also no coincidence that a very high proportion of these hapless souls unintentionally slice, fade or push the ball to the right.

Their vice-like grips make it virtually impossible for the hands and wrists to release properly through impact and leave the clubface pointing right of target as it meets the ball. In fact, some tour professionals and low handicappers incorporate grip pressure in their formula for shaping shots – tight for fades and pushes and loose to encourage very active hands and wrists through impact for draws and pulls. Try it – it could be just the shot-making tip you're looking for.

GRIP NOTE
On a scale of one (very loose) to ten (very tight) the ideal pressure should be four or five.

Grip tight for an open face and a fade.

Grip loosely to promote a closed face and a draw.

MAINLY FOR WOMEN AND JUNIORS

Try baseball style

There are three widely recognised ways of gripping a club – the overlap, the interlock and the baseball.

The overlap and the interlock are used by most men because the hands are 'locked' together by linking the little finger of the right hand and the index finger of the left. This, in effect, means that seven of the eight fingers are in contact with the club.

Because most women's and juniors' hands are smaller and weaker than men's, many teachers recommend they adopt the baseball grip because it means having all the fingers on the grip and therefore more control.

But make sure you do not fall into the trap of gripping the club too tightly, which can lead to all sorts of swing problems. Just let the hands feel the weight of the clubhead and allow the wrists to be flexible enough to allow you to hit freely through impact rather than block it.

The baseball grip is particularly good for small or weak hands.

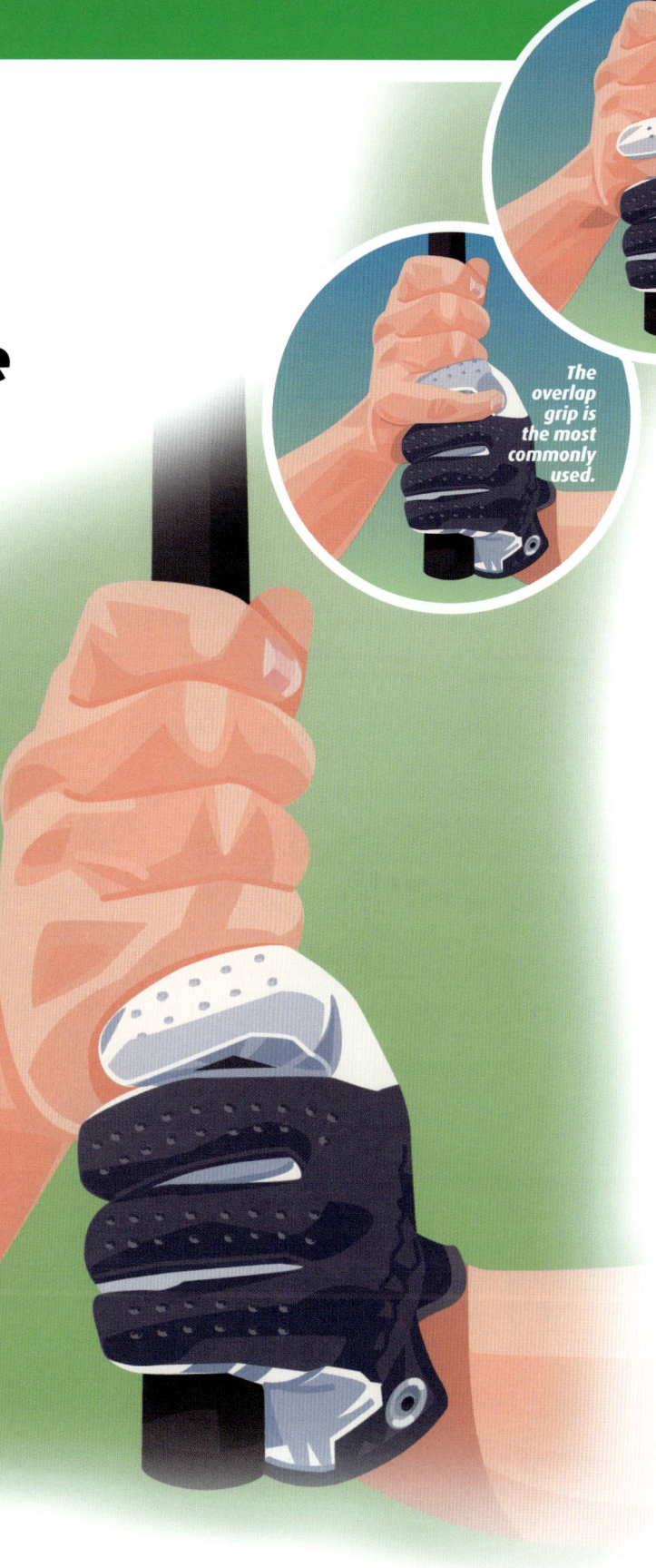

The interlock grip.

The overlap grip is the most commonly used.

17

Fundamentals THE GRIP

THE GRIP

Match up your Vs

Newcomers to the game are often confused about which of the three perfectly acceptable and common grips are suitable for them – the overlapping, interlocking or the baseball (also known as the two-handed).

But there is one golden rule that, according to all the top coaches, you should always observe: when you look down at address, the Vs formed between the thumb and forefinger on each hand should run parallel to each other and point somewhere between the right ear and shoulder.

As long as they line up, you'll be able to hinge them smoothly during the swing.

If they don't, the hands tend to 'fight' each other, making it virtually impossible to hinge either wrist properly going back and release the club with speed and accuracy coming down.

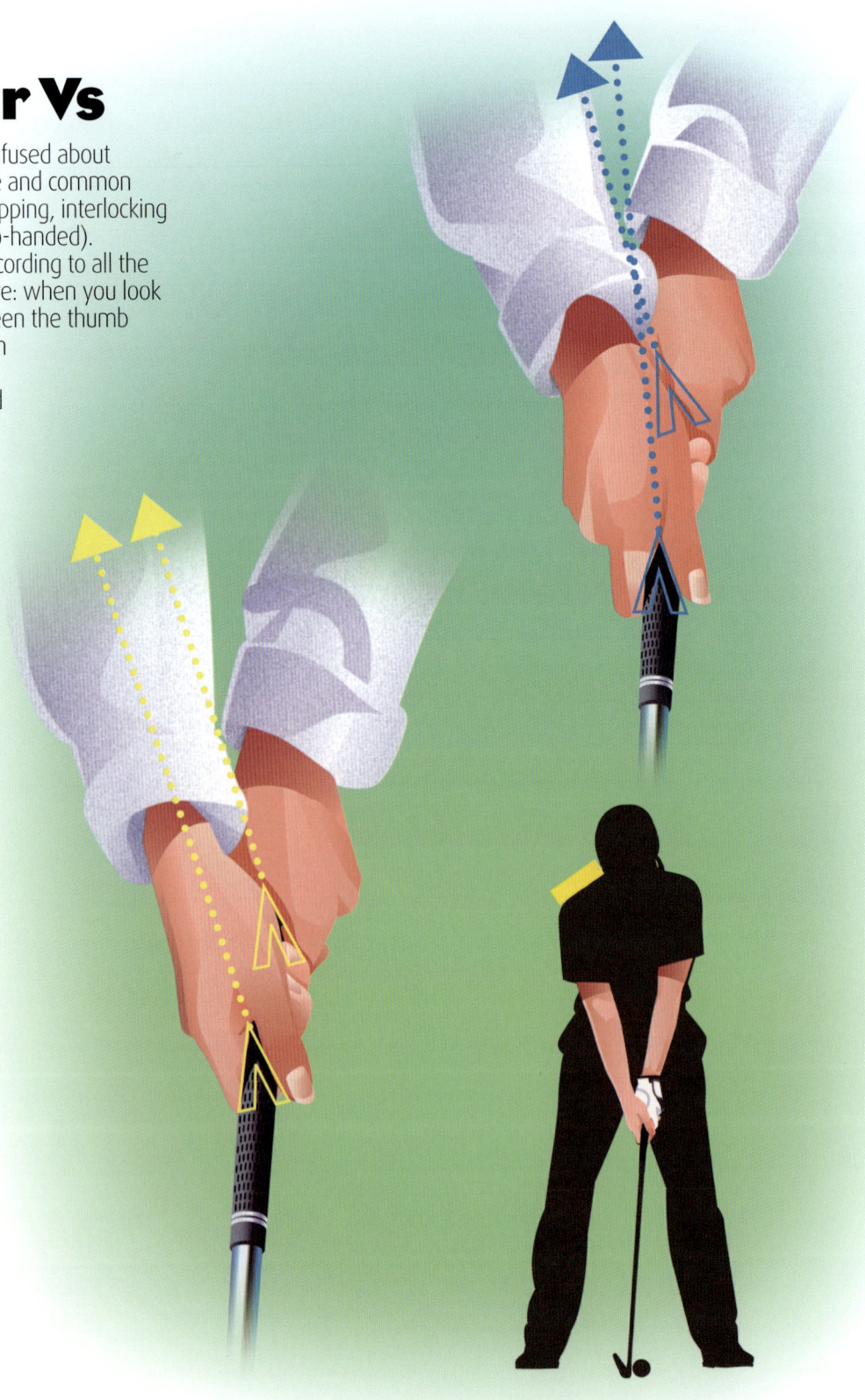

GENERAL PLAY
Backhanded advice!

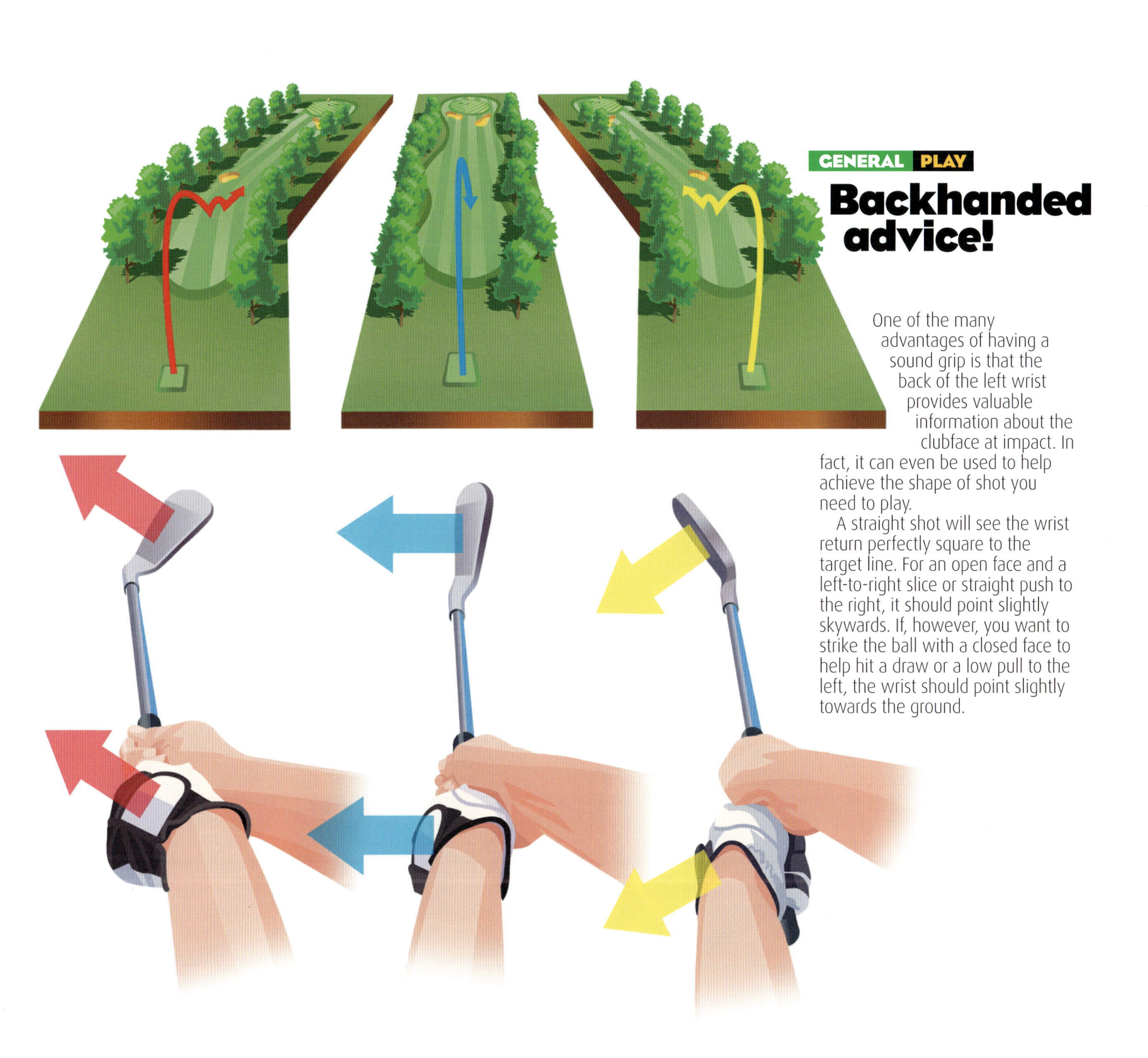

One of the many advantages of having a sound grip is that the back of the left wrist provides valuable information about the clubface at impact. In fact, it can even be used to help achieve the shape of shot you need to play.

A straight shot will see the wrist return perfectly square to the target line. For an open face and a left-to-right slice or straight push to the right, it should point slightly skywards. If, however, you want to strike the ball with a closed face to help hit a draw or a low pull to the left, the wrist should point slightly towards the ground.

19

Fundamentals THE SET-UP

THE SET-UP
Perfect your posture

Most players appreciate the importance of good posture at address and the fact that without it a smooth and repeating swing is virtually impossible to achieve.

One way to find it is, with your heels at shoulder-width apart, to hold the head of a club on top of your head in the left hand and let the shaft run down your back. Take the grip with your right hand against and near the base of the spine.

Retaining the shaft against the spine, bend forward from the hips until you feel your weight move onto your toes. Then flex your knees until your weight comes back to the balls of your feet – and you're there.

The overall position should feel relaxed and athletic with no tension. The chin should also be off the chest.

BALANCED SET-UP
Take the toes test

An excellent way to check that you are standing correctly at address is to make sure you can move your toes up and down inside your shoes.

Avoid having your weight on your toes, as it can lead to all sorts of problems – particularly an out-to-in swingpath through the ball, often leading to a sliced shot.

A well-balanced swing comes from a well-balanced set-up. And this calls for your weight to be evenly distributed on your feet.

TEE TO GREEN

Fundamentals THE SET-UP

THE WOODS

They're not all the same

Left-handers often ask us to remember them when we take photographs for instruction articles, pointing out that they sometimes have difficulty relating the images to their own game. So here's one especially for them:

High and mid-handicappers are recommended to use fairway woods in preference to long irons because they generally get the ball airborne that much easier. But the importance of ball position at address must also be stressed.

Many players believe that ALL the woods should be played with the ball opposite the front heel. Although ideal for the driver (where the ball is swept off a tee peg as the club starts to rise), this is too far forward for the more lofted fairway woods and usually results in topped shots.

If you suffer from this problem, try moving the ball back a couple of inches for the 3-wood and further back still for the 5 and other more lofted woods. You'll be surprised at the improved quality of strike.

STANCE WIDTH
Wide of the mark

In the mistaken belief that they are creating more stability and power, many players stand with their feet too wide at address.

What they are actually doing is inhibiting free motion, creating unwanted tension, restricting weight transfer and forcing themselves to hit at the ball rather than making a nice and fluid swing through it.

Most shots between a drive and a 6-iron call for the heels to be no further apart than the width of the shoulders, gradually narrowing as the lengths of shaft get shorter.

Improve your set-up and you will see an immediate improvement in your tempo, balance and ball-striking.

23

Fundamentals THE SET-UP

1
If your friend can see nothing at all of your front forearm, you are aiming well left of target.

2
If virtually the whole of the inner part of the front forearm is visible, you are standing closed (aiming right of target).

TAKING AIM
What friends are for!

If you think your problems are being caused by poor alignment – and it's amazing how few players do actually get it right – here is a simple way for a friend to stand directly behind you on the target line and check you at address.

3
With just the top of the front forearm showing, you are aligned nice and square to the target line.

BUILD A STANCE

Sit down and stay down

Two of the most common and destructive errors in the game are 'coming up' or 'dipping' during the swing.

If you allow your head and body to rise from their original address positions, the clubhead will return to the ball higher than at address – causing topped and thinned shots.

Conversely, dipping the head and body will result in fat shots or skying the ball.

An excellent mental image to adopt to eliminate both faults is that of sitting on a kitchen or bar stool at address and retaining that posture until after impact.

Incidentally, this image applies to all shots – from a full-blooded drive to a tiddler putt.

25

Fundamentals THE SET-UP

TAKING AIM

Vary the targets on the range

I was chatting with my local pro in the clubhouse bar the other day, when one of the members came in and complained: "I just can't understand it. I was hitting it as straight as an arrow on the range earlier, but was all over the place when I got on the course."

Asked by the pro what flags he was hitting to on the range, the member replied: "The row running straight down the middle."

"It's always best to vary the target when practising," the pro said. "By aiming in the same direction all the time, you are soon able to groove your swing precisely to it. Hitting some balls straight ahead, some to the left and some to the right helps create a much more realistic on-course situation. You only get one attempt at each shot on the course."

BUILD A STANCE

Aim carefully to be a better player

It's amazing how much thought most golfers, especially juniors, give to the mechanics of the swing and yet how little to taking aim. The result is often a beautifully hit shot that flies wide of the target!

The best way to ensure your ball goes where you want it to is to approach from behind and carefully fix the target line. Some players like to point their club directly along the line to get a good feel for the shot.

Now walk up to the ball and place the clubface perfectly square to the target before building your grip and stance round the clubhead. All you have to do is match your excellent aim with an excellent swing!

27

Fundamentals   THE SET-UP

THE SET-UP
Electrifying thought!

The need to build a solid and stable base when playing long shots can be helped by having a mental image of something like an electric pylon when you take up your address position.

Without a firm base from which to hit, you are likely to sway and lose balance through the hitting area, causing weak and inconsistent shots.

The golden rule is to have the inside of the heels (not the out-turned toes) at least as far apart as the tips of your shoulders.

Nick Faldo says he sometimes visualises the Eiffel Tower to remind him to build a stable base.

1 *Place a club across the shoulders and measure the width with your hands.*

THE SET-UP

Foolproof set-up

Here is a very simple and foolproof method of finding the proper stance when you're on the practice ground or at the local driving range. You will soon become accustomed to the feel of the correct distance so that it becomes automatic when you're on the course.

29

Fundamentals THE SET-UP

TAKING AIM

Arm yourself for accuracy

Although most players fully appreciate the importance of aiming correctly – with the feet, hips and shoulders all aligned parallel to the target line – some find it difficult to tell at address whether they are actually on line.

It might look a little odd, but one very effective method is to take up your address position and then lift your left hand off the club. Raise your arm to shoulder height and it will point to where you're actually aiming.

FUNDAMENTALS

Three steps to success

How you stand to the ball at address (known as 'posture') determines the shape of your swing and how you strike the ball.

A good posture sets you in the correct athletic, well-balanced position to allow you to turn your body back and through properly rather than chop into the ball from too high or a flat scything action.

Here's a simple three-step action to help you achieve it:

1 Stand tall and square to the target with your hands on your hips.

2 Flex your knees and bend from the waist.

3 Let your arms hang down loosely in front of you and bring your hands together, making sure your chin is held away from your chest to allow your shoulders to turn under it on the backswing and through-swing.

Fundamentals THE SWING

THE FULL SWING

Make it a 'double chin' check!

Checking that the left shoulder tucks under the chin is a great piece of advice to help achieve a full turn when you make your backswing.

But you rarely hear the shoulders-chin relationship mentioned when it comes to the downswing and followthrough.

Nevertheless, it's a fact that concentrating on your right shoulder tucking under your chin as you pass through and beyond impact helps find the correct in-to-out swingpath and good ball-striking.

One word of warning: make sure you keep everything nice and fluid and don't stiffen up as you start your downswing.

FULL SWING
Shoot from the hip!

A useful key to achieving good distance is turning the right hip early in the backswing.

With the left arm and right hip moving smoothly in unison, the shoulders will automatically turn easily and the club will swing back inside the target line and around the body.

Failure to turn the right hip early in the swing causes the club to travel steeply and outside the line...usually resulting in a weak slice (left-to-right ball flight).

Fundamentals THE SWING

THE TAKEAWAY

Read your palm for a correct takeaway

It's amazing how many shots are consigned to disaster by the time the club has travelled no further than a little beyond parallel to the ground in the backswing.

Here's a very good way of checking whether you are taking the club away from the ball correctly.

Set-up to a ball and swing the club to the point where the shaft is roughly parallel to the ground. Hold the position and use your left hand to take the club carefully out of the right.

If your takeaway action is good, the palm of your right hand will point ahead of you.

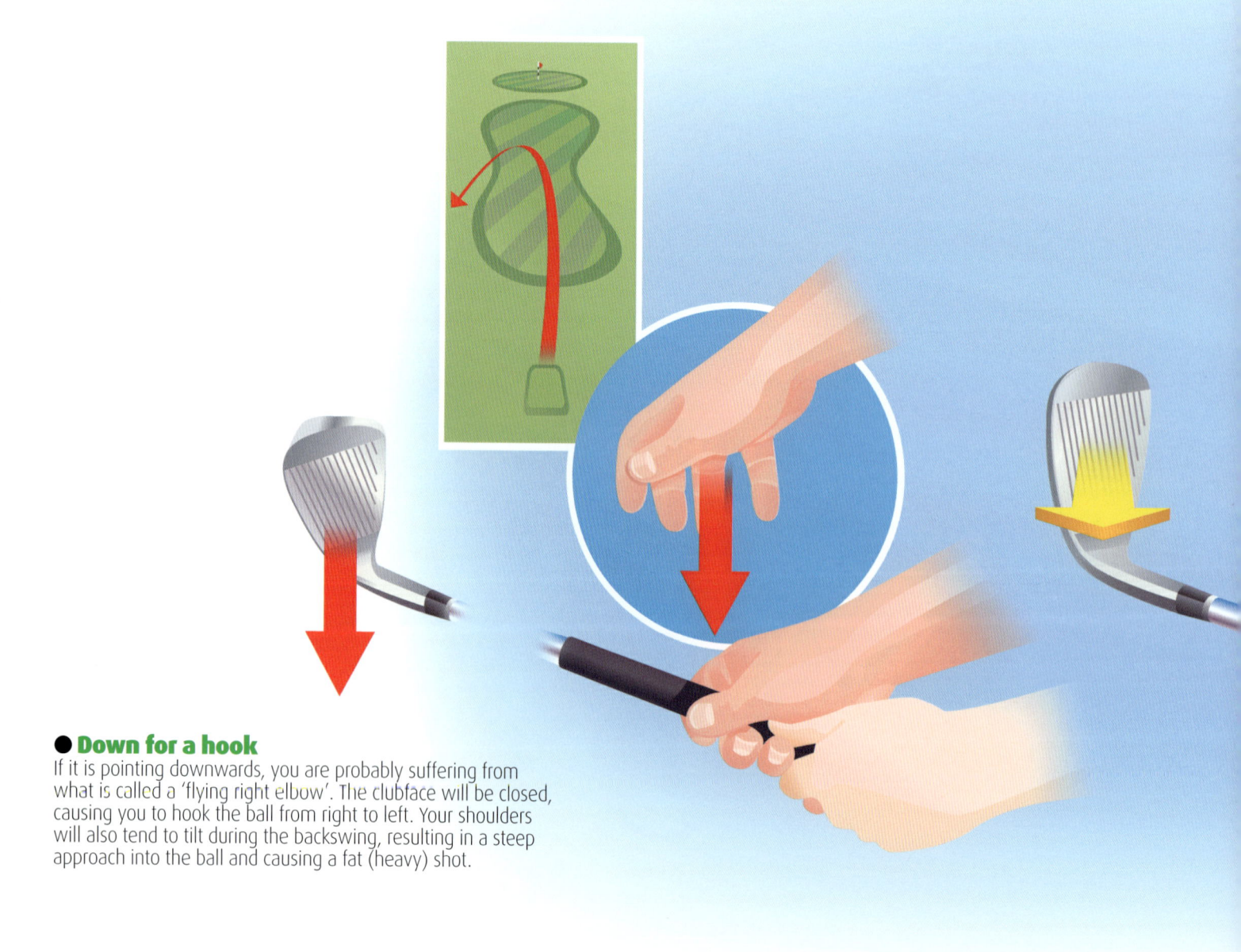

● Down for a hook

If it is pointing downwards, you are probably suffering from what is called a 'flying right elbow'. The clubface will be closed, causing you to hook the ball from right to left. Your shoulders will also tend to tilt during the backswing, resulting in a steep approach into the ball and causing a fat (heavy) shot.

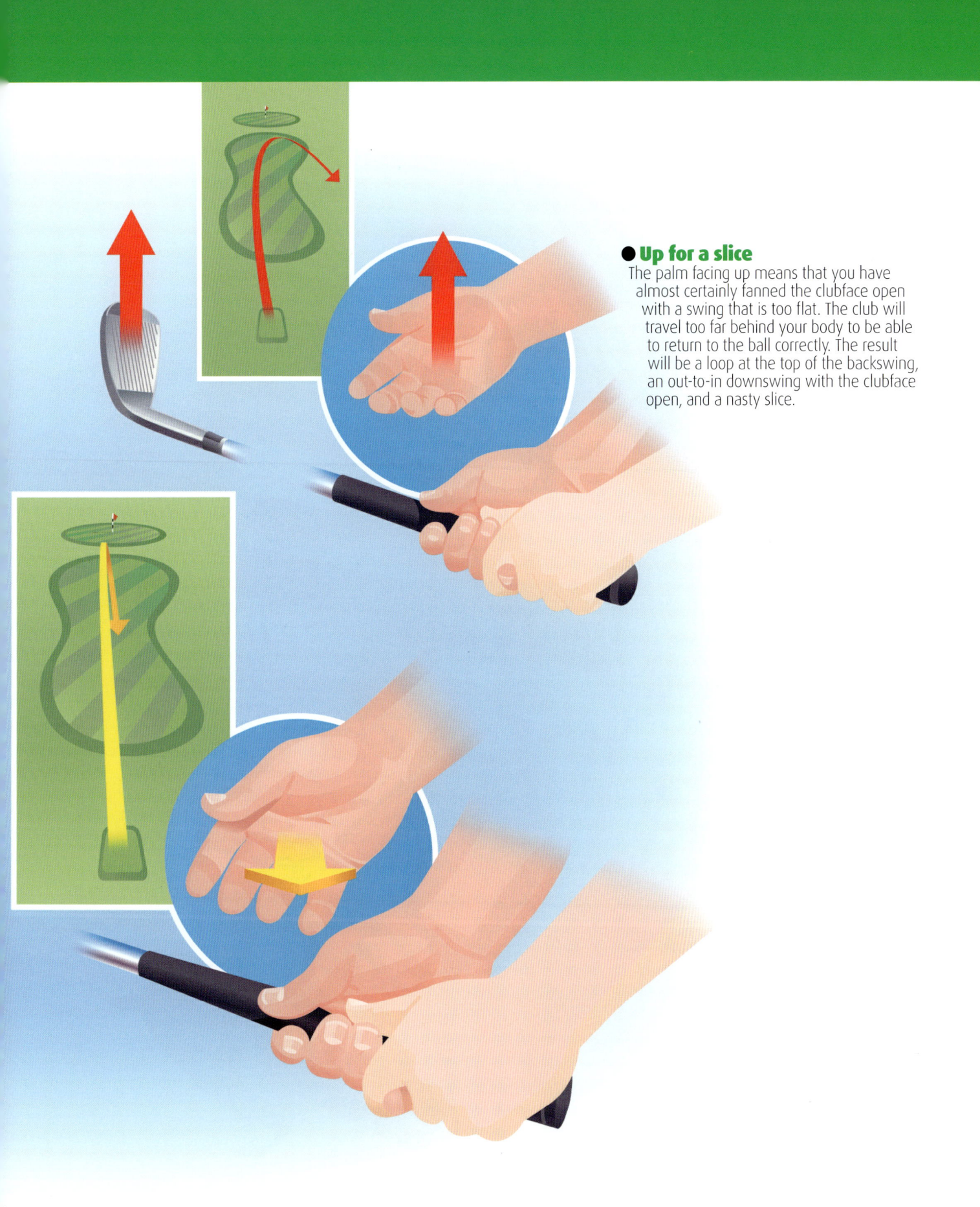

Up for a slice
The palm facing up means that you have almost certainly fanned the clubface open with a swing that is too flat. The club will travel too far behind your body to be able to return to the ball correctly. The result will be a loop at the top of the backswing, an out-to-in downswing with the clubface open, and a nasty slice.

Fundamentals THE SWING

THE SWING
More than just a supporting role

Concentrating on the belt of your trousers when you swing can help eliminate two very common faults – tilting and failing to make a proper finish.

Tilting the upper body, rather than fully turning it, leads to all sorts of problems, including lack of accuracy and power (and you can't get much worse than that!).

This can be avoided by thinking of keeping your belt level with the ground at all points during the swing.

To hit the ball to the intended target, the body must turn through fully. So another useful thought is to make sure the buckle on your belt points directly at the target when you finish.

36

SIMPLE PRACTICE

Don't become a bucket basher

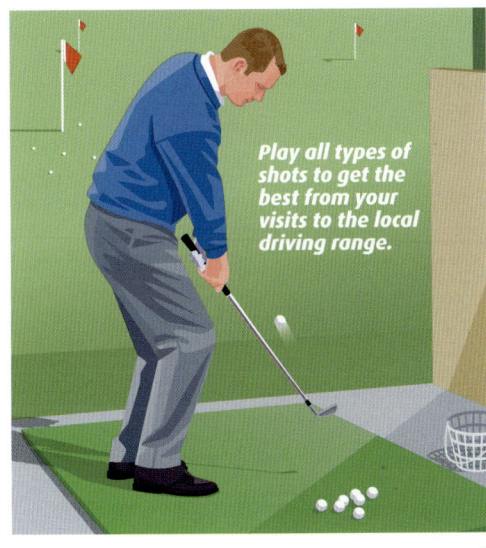

Play all types of shots to get the best from your visits to the local driving range.

Look closely at the vast majority of players at a driving range and you will see them bashing ball after ball with their drivers until the bucket is empty. Apart from loosening a few muscles, they leave no better than when they arrived.

Here's a four-point way of building flexibility and purpose into your practice when you next visit the range.

1 Warm up and work through the clubs, hitting two or three balls with each.

2 Imagine the opening hole at your course and hit the club you normally would from the tee.

3 Assume you have hit your normal distance and dead straight and select the club you would next hit on the hole and use that.

4 Work your way around the course hole by hole, using the full range of clubs you normally would.

And... make sure you spend plenty of time playing bunker shots and putting if the range has these facilities.

Play it by the book

A book makes an excellent guide as to whether you are using your hands and arms correctly and returning the clubhead square to the target line at impact.

Take up your normal address and hold the book with the cover facing upwards. Then swing it to shoulder height, turn your head and check it is still in the same relative position.

Then bring it down to impact and it should be positioned exactly where it started.

The book should return to the same position.

Fundamentals THE SWING

ON THE FAIRWAY
All together now...

A successful swing calls for a smooth one-piece takeaway, with the shoulders, arms and hands all moving together.

Achieve this and the clubhead will automatically stay outside the hands until they reach just before waist height.

An easy way to ensure this happens is to keep the butt end of the club pointing at your belt buckle.

Any independent action will result in it breaking away and facing ahead of you.

GENERAL PLAY

Don't be a heel raiser!

It's a fact that many golfers, particularly those with high handicaps, have trouble controlling the club in the backswing, allowing the clubhead and shaft to drop well beyond parallel at the top. The result is loss of distance and accuracy...not conducive to good scores!

Although grip pressure and a bent left arm often contribute to the fault, the root cause can more times than not be traced to the heel of the front foot.

Allowing it to come well off the ground as you swing back encourages a lifting and tilting action rather than the correct and power-producing turning and coiling movement.

Keep the front heel down, and you'll be delighted at how much better and controlled your swing will feel, and how your ball-striking will improve.

Fundamentals — THE SWING

FROM THE FAIRWAY

Watch the wrists

It's not a bad idea to get a mate to check the position of your left wrist at the top of the swing if you're having trouble keeping the ball straight.

The ideal position to produce a square clubface contact with the ball and a straight hit is where the back of the left wrist is in a straight line with the hand and left arm.

An arched position results in the clubface being returned to the ball in a closed position, usually causing a hook.

In a cupped position at the top, the wrists will return the clubface open to the target line and produce a slice.

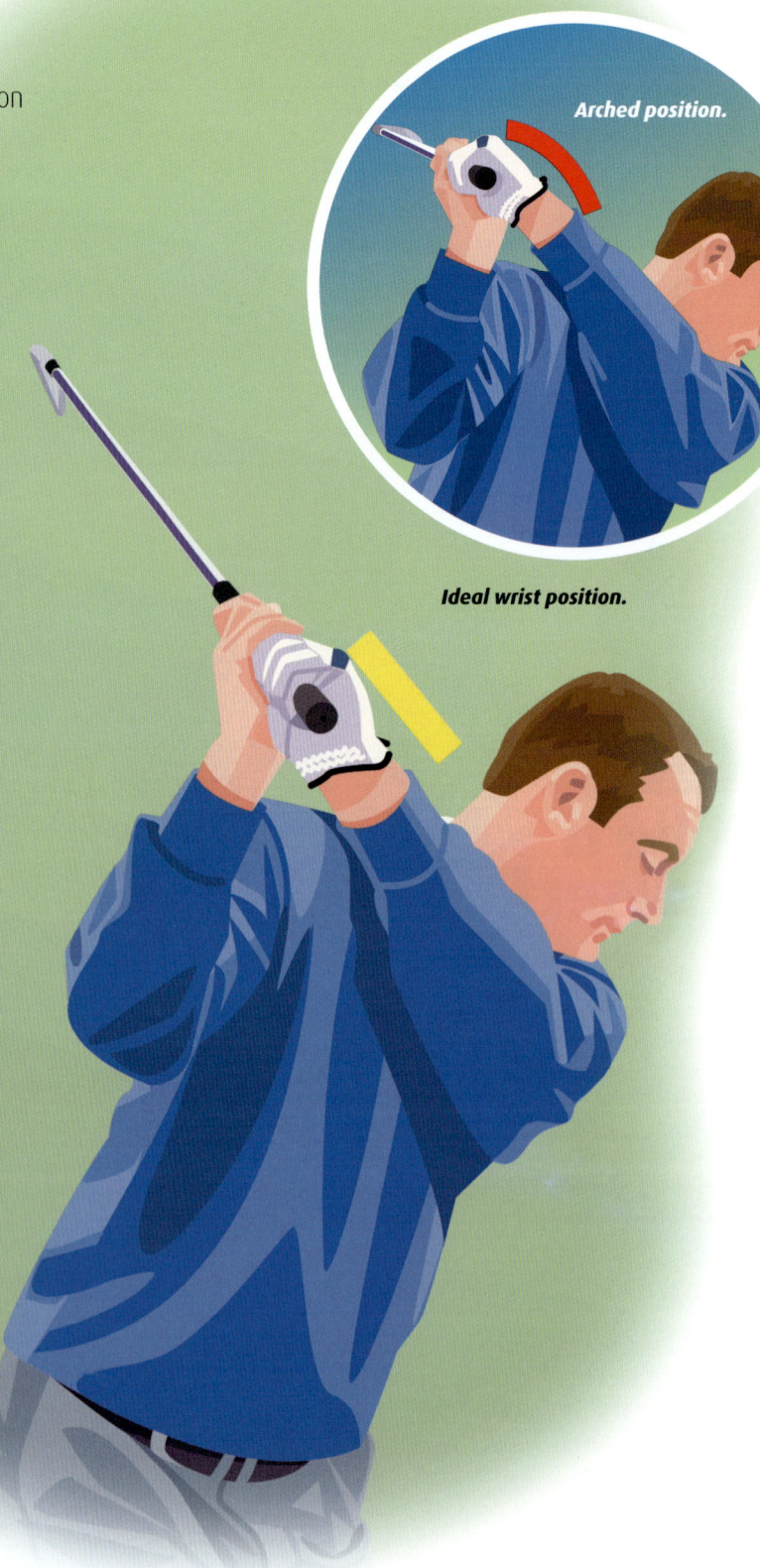

Arched position.

Cupped position.

Ideal wrist position.

GENERAL PLAY

Wind yourself up for good distance

One of the main essentials for powerful action is the creation of a coiling action between the upper body and the legs and hips.

This is achieved by making sure at the top of the swing that the shoulders are turned about twice as much as the hips. The *amount* of turn (often recommended at 45° for the hips and 90° for the shoulders) is not as important as the ratio of two-to-one.

In the correct position at the top, you will feel wound-up and ready to uncoil powerfully down and through impact.

Fundamentals THE SWING

BALANCED SWING

Watch it land

Study any top player in action (amateur or professional) and you will notice that one of the things they all have in common is great balance, whether they are hitting long drives from the tee or playing pitch shots from only 50 yards out.

One way you can achieve a well-balanced swing and build consistency into your game is to concentrate on achieving a good finishing position and then holding it until you see the ball land.

If your swing is anything like that of the typical club player, you'll be surprised how difficult it can be!

WRIST HINGE

Give your swing the thumbs up

Concentrating on the position of your thumbs in the backswing and followthrough can help add both distance and accuracy to your shots.

Pointing both thumbs directly upwards when the arms are roughly parallel with the ground going back (top picture) and through (middle) will ensure you achieve a 90° wrist hinge and find the right swingplane.

It will also improve the release of your wrists through the hitting zone to generate extra clubhead speed and distance.

Most mid and high handicappers 'fan' the clubhead open early in the backswing, causing the thumbs to point more behind them than towards the sky.

43

Fundamentals THE SWING

SWING CHECK
Head for the sun!

A sunny day gives you a golden opportunity (literally!) to check whether you are guilty of moving your head too much when you swing.

By positioning yourself so that the ball sits in the shadow of your head at address, you can see instantly whether there is any excessive lateral or vertical movement from the moment you take the club away from the ball at address right through to the full finish.

Although a little movement to the right is perfectly okay in the backswing, make sure your head does not return at impact to a position forward of where it started. There should be no movement at all up or down between takeaway and impact.

44

FAULT FIXING
Keep your weight under control

In a quest to hit the ball as far as they can off the tee, many golfers – particularly mid and high handicappers – make the big mistake of shifting their weight too far back when they start to swing the club back.

This single fault leads to all sorts of swing problems and poor shots – one of the main combinations being the failure to transfer the weight back towards the front foot on the downswing, leading to topped shots. The result is exactly the reverse of what the player is trying to achieve!

One of the best ways of avoiding this common error is to make sure the right leg is comfortably flexed at address and that the weight is concentrated on the inside of the foot. Hold this position to the top and then down into the ball.

45

Fundamentals MENTAL GAME

PRE-SHOT ROUTINE

See it before you play it

Talk to any good player, amateur or professional, and they will stress the need to visualise a shot before playing it.

In fact, it's very much part of their pre-shot routine and, it is claimed, results in the body automatically responding to the mind's picture of the shot.

That's why, whenever possible, you should approach the ball from directly down the line...it's much easier to 'see' the shot from behind.

So when you are walking to your ball on the fairway, get in line behind it and the target as soon as you can, rather than approaching it from an angle.

As far as tee shots are concerned, it's also a good idea to walk onto the teeing ground from the back rather than the side to get a good perspective of the hole and a visual impression of the shot to be played.

MENTAL GAME
Something to think about

Don't make the common mistake of cluttering your mind with too many swing thoughts when you are out on the course.

In fact, once you have carefully completed your pre-shot routine and are perfectly happy with your set-up, one swing thought is quite enough…whether you're a novice or a really low handicapper. Freeing your mind will free your swing.

If you are currently having lessons, ask your pro what single thought is appropriate and best for you at this stage of your game.

The one-thought policy also works particularly well with trouble shots. For instance, a great one for explosions from greenside bunkers is that you're splashing the ball onto the green on a cushion of sand.

Fundamentals MENTAL GAME

It's as easy as you think!

Here's a very simple mental tip to help the vast number of high handicappers (and, very often, not so high!) who are convinced they are incapable of using long irons and woods.

Imagine that instead of playing what you consider to be a difficult club, you are hitting an easy three-quarter shot into a very large green with a 9-iron or pitching wedge.

By swinging with the same tempo, you will automatically eliminate the root cause of so many bad long-range shots...trying to hit the ball much too hard and thereby losing rhythm and balance.

Think easy and it becomes easy.

An easy swing will produce a nicely balanced finish.

FROM THE FAIRWAY

Just imagine that…

Hitting hard at the ball instead of swinging the clubhead through it is one of the big mistakes made by most amateurs. The result is usually a poor shot accompanied by an ugly, off-balance finish.

A good mental image to help you swing through the ball is another ball on the target line and about six inches ahead of the one you are about to play.

After striking the real ball, go on to strike the imaginary one. It will help you to achieve a full and nicely balanced finish with all your weight on the front foot.

Imagine there's a ball ahead of the real one.

The result is a full and nicely balanced finish.

This ugly finish is the result of hitting at the ball rather than through it.

49

Fundamentals   MENTAL GAME

PRE-ROUND PRACTICE

'Play' the first hole before you start!

Are you one of the many poor souls who always seem to make a complete botch of the opening hole? If so, there is a way to prepare physically and mentally for those crucial first two or three shots.

Before ending your warm-up session on the practice ground, spend the last few minutes playing the shots needed on the opening hole.

For instance, if the tee shot demands a right-to-left ball flight to keep you out of trouble, imagine you're actually on the tee and play a few draws until you feel completely comfortable with the shape.

Then go on and rehearse playing the second shot – perhaps a high one over trouble with plenty of backspin to prevent it running into more trouble behind the green.

You can now walk to the first tee knowing that you've given yourself a good chance of getting your round off to a flying start.

51

Fundamentals — MENTAL GAME

THE FULL SWING

Rollercoast your way to a full swing

Many top players admit to using various mental images to help them achieve certain swing positions or play particular shots. Here's a picture to have in your mind to cover the entire swing, from the set-up to the followthrough.

Simply think of the whole thing as a ride on a rollercoaster, with six distinct golfing images tied in to the scene.

1 Take up a nice, comfortable position in the car ready for the action ahead (in golf, this equates to a relaxed address).

4 Brakes off as the car begins its swift descent (accelerate the club down smoothly into the hitting zone).

5 We're screaming! (The clubhead reaches its maximum speed at impact with the ball.)

52

2▸

The car makes its slow, smooth climb to the top (smooth backswing).

3◂

The car comes to a virtual standstill at the top (don't snatch the club down).

6▸

The car slows down as it starts to rise again (the followthrough).

53

Fundamentals SHOT MAKING

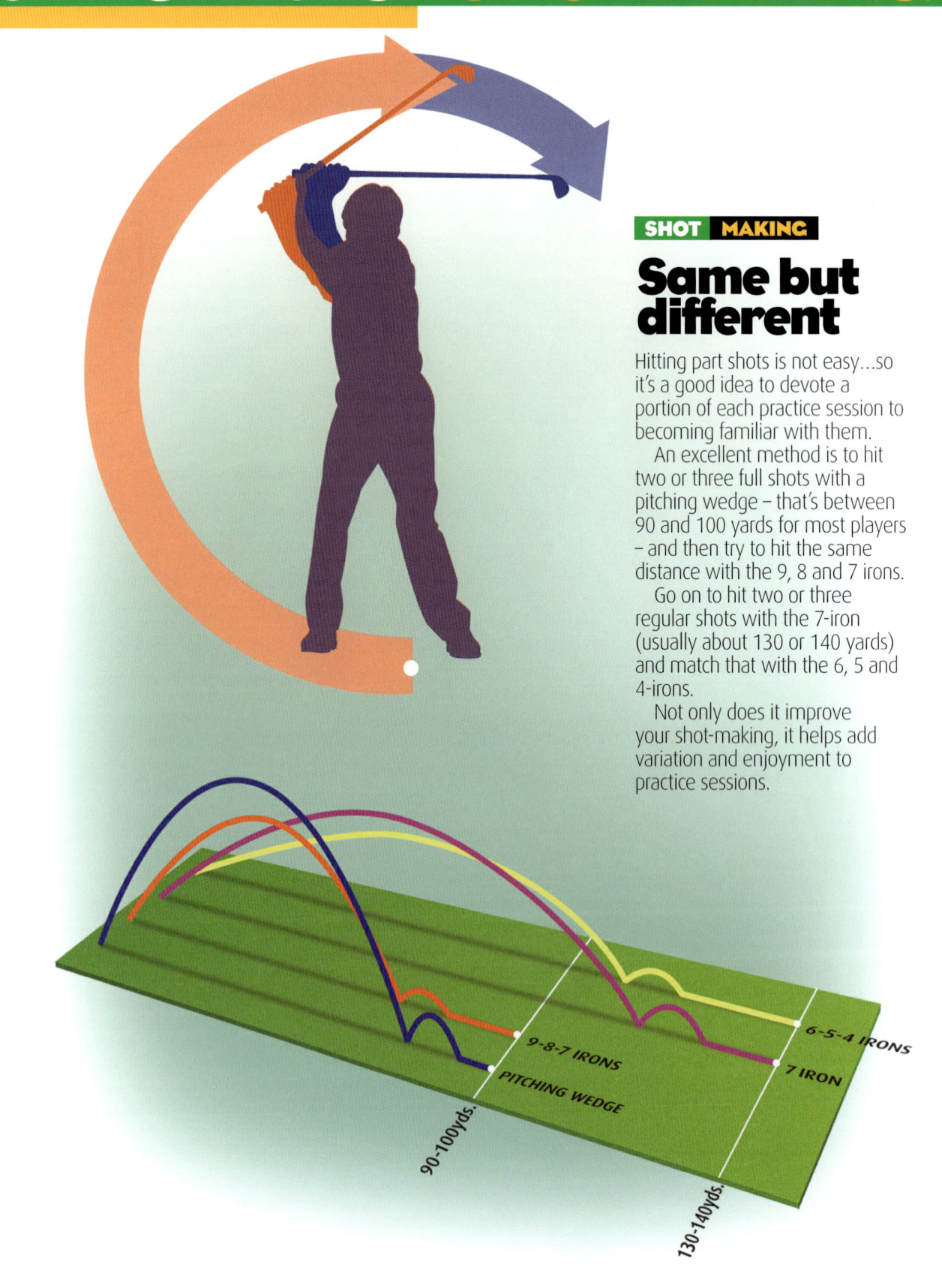

SHOT MAKING

Same but different

Hitting part shots is not easy...so it's a good idea to devote a portion of each practice session to becoming familiar with them.

An excellent method is to hit two or three full shots with a pitching wedge – that's between 90 and 100 yards for most players – and then try to hit the same distance with the 9, 8 and 7 irons.

Go on to hit two or three regular shots with the 7-iron (usually about 130 or 140 yards) and match that with the 6, 5 and 4-irons.

Not only does it improve your shot-making, it helps add variation and enjoyment to practice sessions.

PITCHING WEDGE — 90-100yds.
9-8-7 IRONS
7 IRON — 130-140yds.
6-5-4 IRONS

GENERAL PLAY

Better by half!

Most amateurs, particularly high handicappers, have difficulty mastering part shots with their irons…and certainly rarely practise them. Yet it's surprising how often they are called upon to play less-than-full shots during a round.

A good way to improve shot-making skills without visiting the practice ground is to go onto the course every now and again and play the first nine holes with only the odd-numbered clubs and the inward nine with the even numbered. Reverse the procedure next time you go out.

Most players will be surprised how soon they learn to improvise with different clubs – and how much fun they can have doing so.

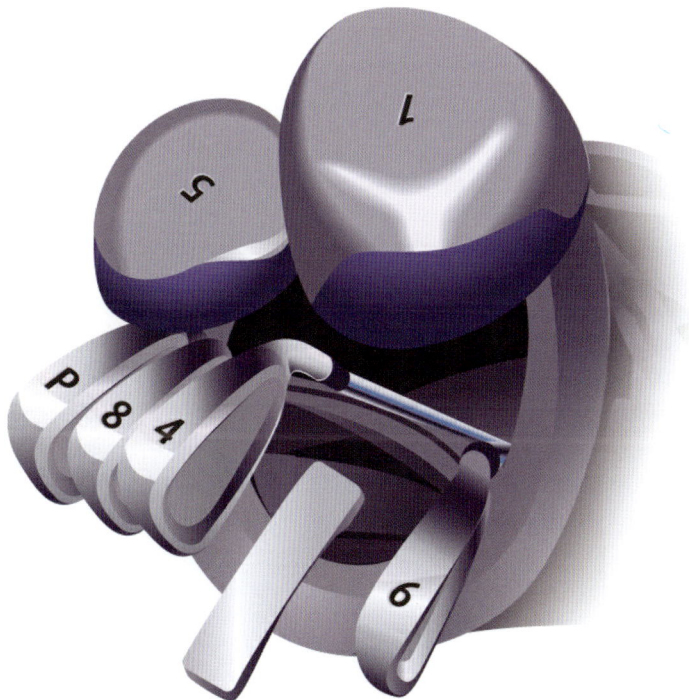

Fundamentals WEIGHT TRANSFER

WEIGHT TRANSFER
Pointed evidence

Failing to transfer weight from the back to the front foot through the hitting zone is one of the most common faults in golf and leads to a multitude of poor shots, including topping and the slice. Try this check to see if your action passes the test:

Play a ball off a tee peg and then hold your finishing position. Let the club you're using hang naturally from the right shoulder and see where the head points.

If it's ahead of the peg you've come through the test with flying colours. Behind means you're failing to shift your weight forward.

FAULT FIXING

THE SHANK

Simply effective

Ask any player who knows a thing or two about golf what's the most soul-destroying shot in the game and it's a safe bet the reply will be 'the shank'.

Many thousands of words have been devoted over the years on the causes and how to cure the shot where the ball is struck off the hosel (the part of the club where the shaft joins the head) and shoots off at a sharp angle to the right.

The most simple and effective cure I have ever come across is to address the ball off the heel (shank) of the clubhead and then concentrate on striking it off the toe.

Although you have my word that it works, I really hope you don't need to put it to the test!

TARGET LINE

Fundamentals FAULT FIXING

THE SLICE

A real 'belter' to cure your slice

One of the most common mistakes by club golfers, especially when using the long clubs, is what is termed 'hitting from the top'.

As a result, the right shoulder leads the downswing and the clubhead travels through the hitting area on an out-to-in path to produce a nasty slice.

One way to help prevent this is to concentrate on the position of your belt buckle. At address, it should face straight ahead of you and at right angles to the target line. Then you should concentrate on getting it to face directly at the target as you swing through to a full followthrough.

Concentrating on the buckle, in effect, helps make your lower half the dominant factor in the downswing, rather than that faulty right shoulder.

GLOVE TALK

Handy reminder

How many times have you come in from a poorly played round of golf and cursed the fact that, in the heat of competitive play, you forgot to do what you'd been working on all week to improve your game? If you're typical of the average keen golfer, the answer is many times.

A great way to prevent this happening is to write on your glove (or, if you don't use one, the back of your hand) a simple reminder.

A short message – like 'light grip', 'slow back' or 'full turn' – will jump at you every time you address the ball.

You'll never remember to do it!

Fundamentals CONSISTENT PLAY

Give your bad shots the elbow

Keeping the elbows the same distance apart from address right through to the finish is a favourite piece of advice from experienced teaching professionals. Loss of control usually occurs when the elbows move apart or closer together during the swing. Most novices and high handicappers allow their elbows to move further apart rather than closer together.

Reach for the safer option

Lofted fairway woods, with their large heads and broad soles, are, for the vast majority of players, a much safer bet for consistency than the 3 and 4-irons. Not only is it harder to get the ball into the air with long irons, but they also create more sidespin than backspin, causing hooks and slices.

Don't go flat out for trouble

Never swing flat out. About 75% of your maximum speed for full shots with every club is about right and will prevent you losing balance and hitting the ball all over the place. Some players benefit by imagining there are poles stuck in the ground against the outside of their feet and that they have to avoid making any contact with them either in the backswing or followthrough.

100%

75%

61

Fundamentals COMPETITION

WINNING TACTICS Good course management and an intelligent strategy will ensure you will rarely be called upon to play shots beyond your capabilities. Here are some tips to help you lift a few trophies this year:

● **Keep your eye on** what club your opponent is using. Remember, there's no penalty for looking – but you are not allowed to move clubs in their bag to obtain information.

● **Carefully watch** your opponent's line and pace of putts. Not paying close attention could rob you of the opportunity of discovering match-winning information about the green.

● **Keep them guessing** when it comes to conceding short putts. Give some, by all means, but not all. Being asked to putt a tricky short one after several concessions can be quite nerve-racking.

62

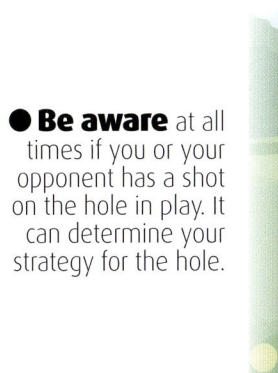

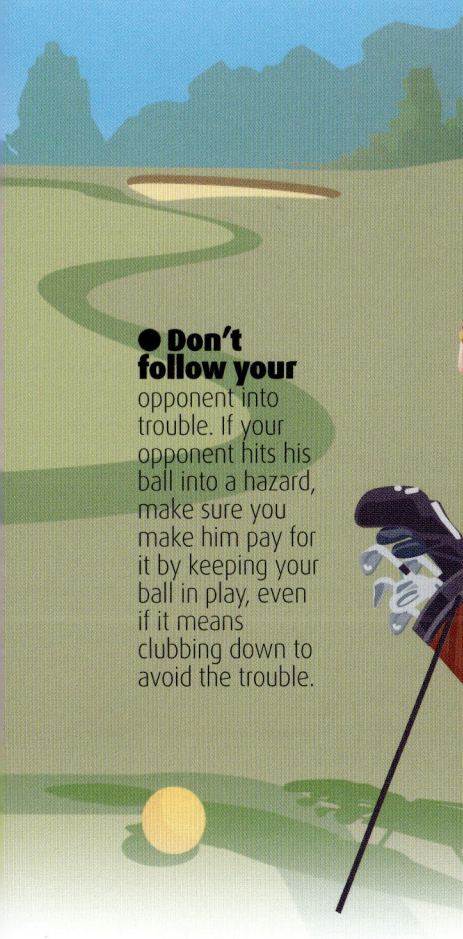

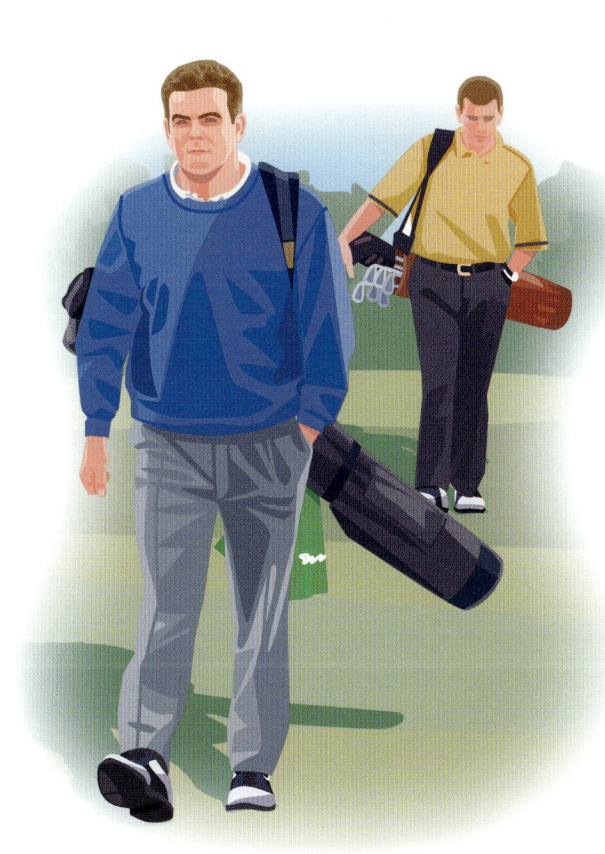

- **Be aware** at all times if you or your opponent has a shot on the hole in play. It can determine your strategy for the hole.

- **Don't follow your** opponent into trouble. If your opponent hits his ball into a hazard, make sure you make him pay for it by keeping your ball in play, even if it means clubbing down to avoid the trouble.

- **Don't allow** your opponent to disrupt the normal pace at which you play. It's an old matchplay ploy. Always play at your own pace.

Fundamentals   HIT IT FURTHER

GO FOR DISTANCE Asking a golfer if he wants to hit the ball further is akin to asking a starving man if he fancies a free slap-up meal. So here are half-a-dozen simple and proven tips that could help you hit the ball a few yards past your mates' best drives.

● See the knuckles
Make sure at address that you can see at least three knuckles of the left hand and the Vs formed between the index fingers and thumbs point to the right shoulder. This is what is called a strong grip and helps to ensure the clubface is square or a fraction closed to the target line at impact to give maximum distance.

● Point the shoulder
In order to complete a full and powerful turn of the upper body, ensure at the top of the swing that your left shoulder points at the ball. Holding your chin off your chest at address will create a slot for the shoulder to pass under.

● Resistance is useful
Create a power coil action by resisting the turning motion of the upper body with your legs to avoid lateral sway. Concentrate particularly during the backswing on keeping your right knee flexed and your weight inside the right foot. Practising with a ball or club under the outside of the back foot helps achieve this.

Correct.

Wrong.

● Release the hands
The hands need to be fully released through the hitting area to achieve maximum clubhead speed. Avoid a blocking action by trying to turn the palm of the right hand over the left wrist.

● Check the flex
A surprising number of amateurs play with equipment ill-suited to their swings. Seek out your local PGA-qualified professional and get him or her to check the flex of the shafts and the loft and lie of the heads to determine whether they are giving you maximum performance. Also ask about what type of ball you should be using.

R-FLEX

● Back low and slow
Taking the clubhead away from the ball low and slow helps to create a wide swing arc – one of the essentials for fast clubhead speed (and therefore distance). Some players like to adopt a mental image of a ball just back of the right foot and pushing it back a few inches with the back of the clubhead.

65

Practice SWING

GENERAL PLAY
Build a bridge for balance

One of the essential ingredients of a grooved golf swing is good balance. And here's an excellent drill to help you achieve it:

Get a couple of bricks and a short length of wood thick enough to bear your weight.

Lay the wood across the bricks and then step onto the middle of it and take up your normal address posture.

Start by making some gentle swings with a short or mid-iron and then build up until you can comfortably complete full swings without falling off the wood.

Retain a mental image of swinging on your home-built 'bridge' when you are playing shots on the course.

ON THE FAIRWAY

Firm up your ball striking

Here's an excellent practice drill to prevent your leading side collapsing through impact, causing loss of power and accuracy.

Position your bag of clubs on the ground so you can push the outside of your leading foot hard up against it and hit shots. The bag should provide enough resistance to prevent the foot sliding forward and the leg collapsing.

Out on the course, you can set your foot up against tee boxes or markers.

Practice SWING

SWINGPATH CHECK

Strip the bed for a better swing!

If you slice or pull the ball (and, be honest, most of you do!), it's virtually certain that the swingpath of the clubhead through the hitting zone is from out to in.

You can easily check if this is so by pegging an old sheet or blanket to a washing line and swinging a club at a tee in the ground a few inches to the side.

The object is to sweep the peg away without striking the sheet either before or after impact on a correct in-to-square-to-in path.

Any contact with the sheet before the clubhead reaches the peg is proof that it is coming into the impact zone from the outside.

Contact with the sheet after the strike means your path has been in-to-out, usually resulting in a shot pushed to the right or a hook.

COURSE MANAGEMENT

ON THE FAIRWAY

Find your own answer

Here's a simple way of finding the answer to one of the questions most often asked by mid and high handicappers: "Should I use a 3-iron or a lofted wood for long shots off the fairway?"

Take 20 white and 20 yellow balls of the same quality onto the practice ground and hit one colour with the iron and the other with the wood. To prevent boredom and ensure a really fair test, it's best to hit them in five-ball batches rather than all 20 of one colour consecutively.

Keep going until a definite pattern emerges on consistency, length and accuracy. You can then choose between the two.

Incidentally, it's worth repeating the test every few months to make sure things haven't changed.

Practice COURSE MANAGEMENT

Prepare yourself for what's ahead

It's always a good idea when playing a course for the first time to arrive well before your tee-off time, pick up a course planner or scorecard, and have a word with the local professional or his assistant.

Information on the general length of the holes, the type of sand in the bunkers, severity of rough and the density and variety of trees can then form the basis of your pre-round practice session.

If, for instance, there are several long par 3s and 4s, you should devote some time hitting fairway woods and long irons.

Narrow tree-lined fairways will almost certainly call for some low punches with your long and mid-irons, and shots from the practice bunkers will help gauge the amount of sand you need to take and the best angle of attack for success.

Finally, get to know the pace of the greens. Time spent on the practice green invariably results in strokes saved early in the round.

BEATING BOREDOM
Become a fantasy champion!

Ask most mid and high handicappers why they don't practise as much as they know they should and it's a fairly safe bet that the vast majority will reply, "Because it's too boring."

One of the best mental exercises I know to combat the problem is to try to picture in your mind a shot to a particular famous hole and then imagine you're playing it there and then in a major competition.

How about, for instance, the drive at the tantalising 10th on the Brabazon course at The Belfry, or a splash shot from the treacherous greenside bunker guarding the Road Hole (17th) on the Old Course at St Andrews?

Before long, you'll be winning more fantasy Majors than you ever dreamed of. And there's nothing boring about that!

Practice COURSE MANAGEMENT

FROM THE FAIRWAY

On the high side

Most players have a fairly good idea of how far they hit each of their clubs (including the carry) in normal weather conditions.

But it's surprising how few know how HIGH they hit the ball and their rates of climb.

This information is, of course, crucial if you have to play a shot over a tree or under some branches.

It's a good idea when you next practice to set aside a little time to gauge just how high you hit each club. It could save you hearing that horrible sound of ball striking timber next time you're out on the course.

PRACTICE PLAN

Look back for the future

When poor weather won't allow you on the course, snuggle down in your favourite armchair with a notebook and pen and replay in your mind some of your recent rounds.

Cast your mind back carefully and you are bound to discover that certain shots repeatedly caused particular pain and prevented your handicap from coming down as much as it could have done.

Once the list is complete, you will know exactly where your attention should be directed on the practice ground and driving range.

Practice FUNDAMENTALS

Throw 10 or 12 balls into a bunker and play them where they come to rest. Vary the distances you go for.

Devote at least 15 balls to playing into the green from those awkward distances between about 30 yards and your normal length for a full sand wedge. Again, vary the clubs.

Hit 20 or 25 balls with your long and mid irons and fairway woods. Again, don't hit consecutive balls with the same club and try a few controlled fades and draws with the long irons.

BEAT BOREDOM

Improve your game ...with interest

It's surprising how many golfers say "I want to improve my game but find practising so boring.

Most players make the mistake of going to their practice ground and hitting all their shots – whether they be full drives or short chips – from the same spot and in the same direction. No wonder they become bored!

Unless you need to concentrate on one or two particular departments of the game, give the following varied programme a try. We're sure you'll leave the practice ground still mentally fresh and with an improved game.

● **Keen for more?**
Go to the putting green and hit putts from varying distances until you feel your concentration beginning to wane. It's then time to head home...or the bar.

74

Hit 20 chip shots from varying distances and using different clubs around the practice green. Don't hit consecutive balls from the same spot with the same club.

Find some rough and play six or eight balls from progressively difficult lies. Concentrate on simply getting the ball out rather than going for distance.

Find a nasty divot and play three or four balls from it. Remember to position the ball well back in your stance and hit down and through to create another divot within the divot.

Practice FUNDAMENTALS

SIMPLE PRACTICE Want to brush up and check your game but haven't enough time to get to your local club or driving range? Don't despair...all is not lost. A walk into the back garden with some clubs, balls and a few items from the shed or laying about are all you need to complete some valuable work before darkness falls or you are called away from the important things in life.

- **Hitting low chips** under a patio table or bench helps rid you of flicking at the ball with the wrists (causing loss of accuracy and distance control) and encourages the correct action for those crucial greenside shots.

- **An upturned umbrella** makes the perfect target for short pitch and lob shots. But don't hit your shots all from the same spot – remember you only get one chance when you're out on the course. Vary the length and angles of your shots.

- **The handle of a brush** placed under the outside of the right foot encourages the right knee to remain flexed and create resistance of the lower body against the coil of the upper body during the backswing. These two factors, of course, create the major source of power in the swing

76

● **Patio or garden path slabs** are excellent for checking alignment and ball position. Also use the lines to examine whether the swingpath of the clubhead away from the ball is correct and your putting line is okay.

● **A spade** placed a few inches behind the ball will help ensure the necessary steep angle of attack for chip shots. This path into the ball is needed to achieve a ball-then-turf contact.

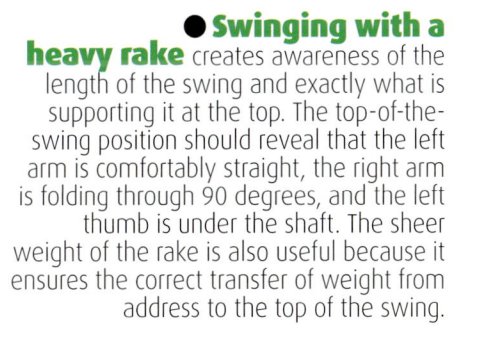

● **Swinging with a heavy rake** creates awareness of the length of the swing and exactly what is supporting it at the top. The top-of-the-swing position should reveal that the left arm is comfortably straight, the right arm is folding through 90 degrees, and the left thumb is under the shaft. The sheer weight of the rake is also useful because it ensures the correct transfer of weight from address to the top of the swing.

77

Practice FUNDAMENTALS

PLANE CHECK
Many happy returns

Most experienced players appreciate that one of the basics of good golf is to return the club at impact to its position at address. But how can you check if you're doing this correctly?

Answer: set up to the ball with a club and get a friend to push two canes or clubshafts into the ground about eight inches apart and on a plane parallel to your club – one just outside the ball and the other just inside your hands.

Then go ahead and hit some balls. Any contact with the two canes or shafts will underline the fact that things are not quite as they should be.

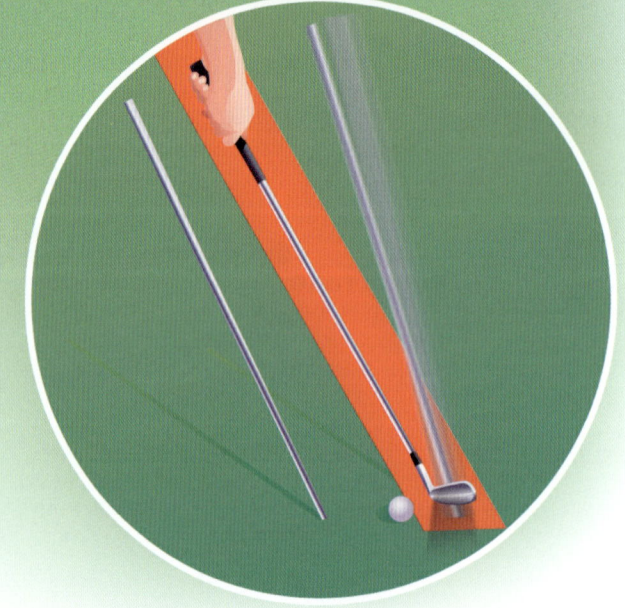

78

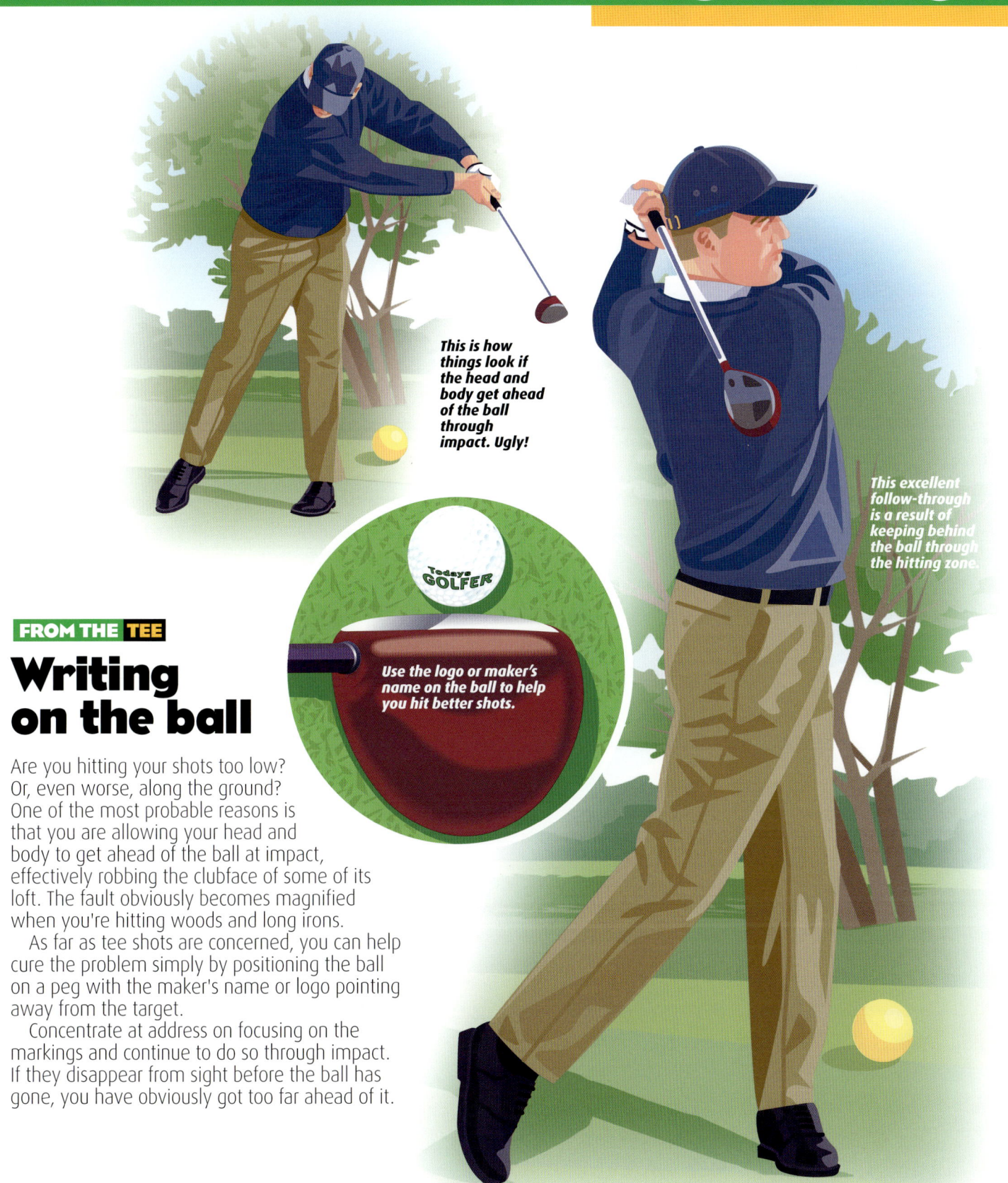

From the tee

This is how things look if the head and body get ahead of the ball through impact. Ugly!

This excellent follow-through is a result of keeping behind the ball through the hitting zone.

Use the logo or maker's name on the ball to help you hit better shots.

FROM THE TEE
Writing on the ball

Are you hitting your shots too low? Or, even worse, along the ground? One of the most probable reasons is that you are allowing your head and body to get ahead of the ball at impact, effectively robbing the clubface of some of its loft. The fault obviously becomes magnified when you're hitting woods and long irons.

As far as tee shots are concerned, you can help cure the problem simply by positioning the ball on a peg with the maker's name or logo pointing away from the target.

Concentrate at address on focusing on the markings and continue to do so through impact. If they disappear from sight before the ball has gone, you have obviously got too far ahead of it.

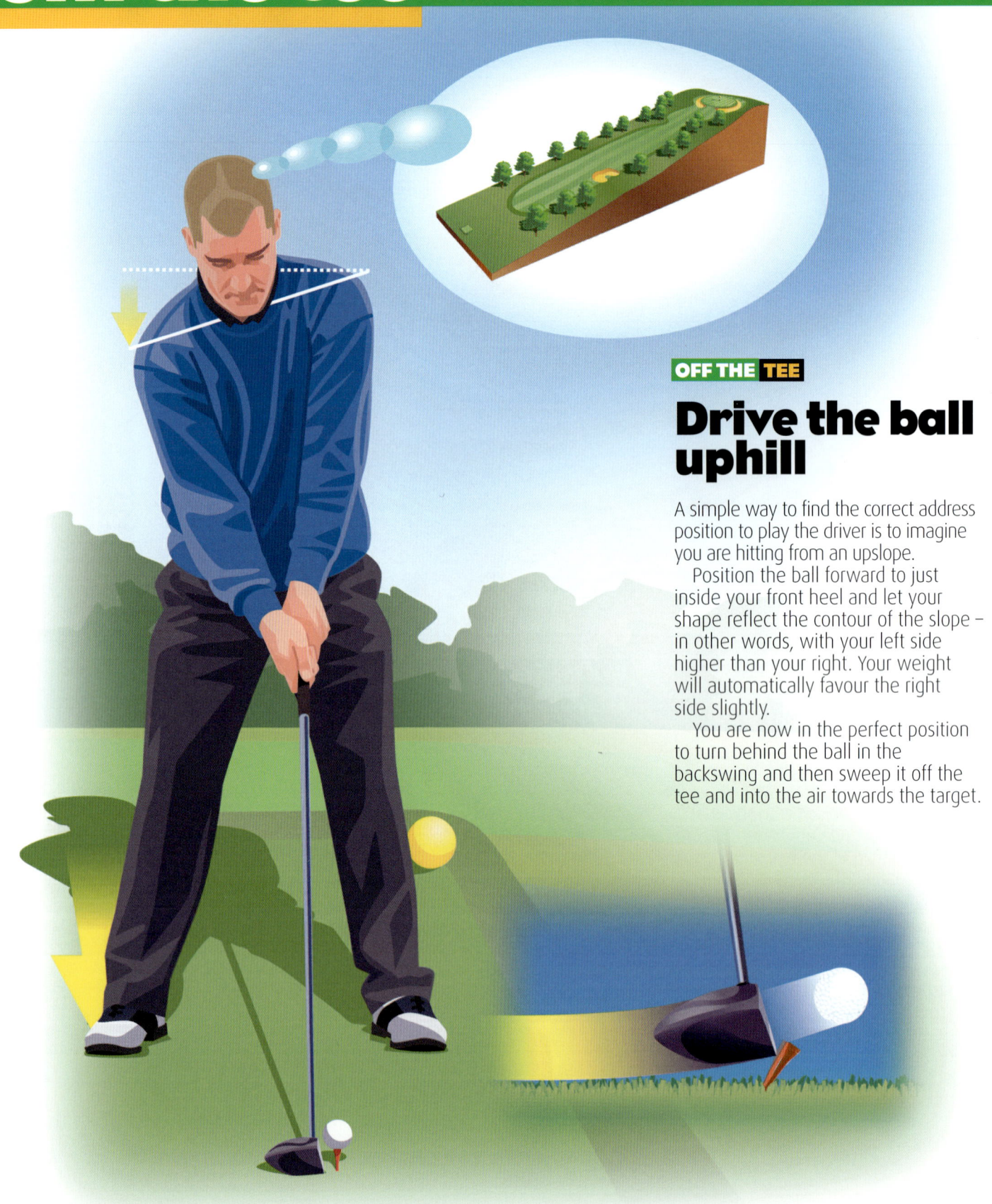

From the tee

OFF THE TEE

Drive the ball uphill

A simple way to find the correct address position to play the driver is to imagine you are hitting from an upslope.

Position the ball forward to just inside your front heel and let your shape reflect the contour of the slope – in other words, with your left side higher than your right. Your weight will automatically favour the right side slightly.

You are now in the perfect position to turn behind the ball in the backswing and then sweep it off the tee and into the air towards the target.

TEE TO GREEN

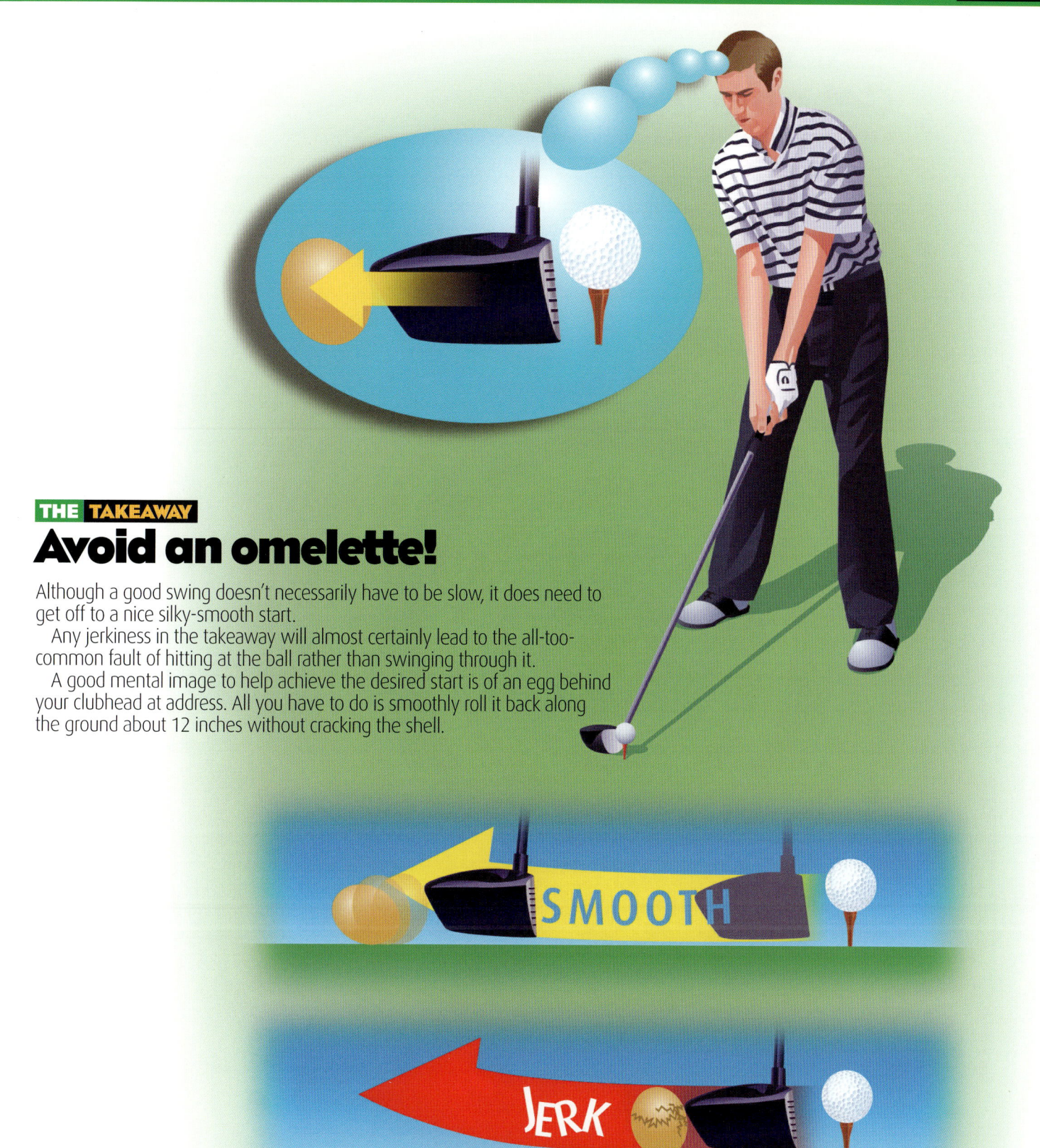

THE TAKEAWAY
Avoid an omelette!

Although a good swing doesn't necessarily have to be slow, it does need to get off to a nice silky-smooth start.

Any jerkiness in the takeaway will almost certainly lead to the all-too-common fault of hitting at the ball rather than swinging through it.

A good mental image to help achieve the desired start is of an egg behind your clubhead at address. All you have to do is smoothly roll it back along the ground about 12 inches without cracking the shell.

From the tee

FROM THE TEE

Get on track

Have you wondered why you can strike shot after shot straight down the middle of the driving range but then hit the ball embarrassingly all over the place once you're out on a real golf course?

Apart from the obvious matter of pressure and tension, one of the other main causes is often the fact that the side panels of driving range bays offer perfect alignment aids.

So next time you are out on the course, simply imagine you are at the range and the side panels are extending like railway lines each side of the target.

FROM THE TEE

Chain reaction

Are you a snatcher? In other words, one of the many high handicappers who jerk the clubhead away from the ball much too quickly and therefore ruin any chance of a smooth and well-balanced swing.

If you are, imagine there is a heavy metal ball attached to the clubhead by a thick iron chain. Slowly take up the slack on the chain and then pull the ball back smoothly to get it rolling.

Pulling the clubhead away slowly from address helps to ensure the necessary one-piece takeaway between club, hands, arms and body and a much smoother tempo.

This mental image will help ensure a smooth start to your swing.

Around the green

GREENSIDE TACTICS

So long, so good!

Unless there's serious trouble behind the green or you'll leave yourself with a really nasty downhill putt, there are two very good reasons why you should *always* aim to chip the ball beyond the hole.

The first is, of course, that you cannot possibly hole the shot if the ball pulls up short.

The second is a little more practical. Watching the path of the ball beyond the hole provides valuable information on borrows and pace for the putt back. So look carefully!

TEE TO GREEN

Focus on a spot a couple of inches ahead of the ball...

... and keep looking at it until the ball is well on its way to the target.

AROUND THE GREEN

Take a full frontal view

The thinned chip from the fringe of the green has got to be right up there on the list of the most annoying and frustrating shots in golf. Instead of playing the ball close to the pin to save a par, you're suddenly staring down the barrel of a double-bogey.

One of the most common faults is failing to stay down on the shot. Anxious to see where the ball is going, you look up – causing the shoulders to rise and the club to strike the top half of the ball. Your next shot is a similar chip from the other side of the green.

Here's a simple way of solving the problem. Instead of focussing on the ball at address, look at a spot a couple of inches in front of it and keep looking there until the clubhead has passed through. Your next job is to pick the ball out of the hole or tap it in from a few inches!

Incidentally, this tip also works perfectly well on putts.

85

Around the green

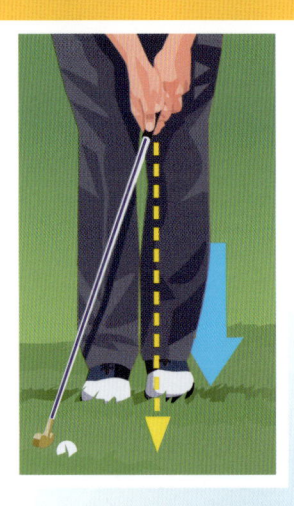

FROM THE FRINGE

Pop goes the problem!

Do you automatically reach for the sand iron when your ball is lying well down in a deep fringe of grass around the green...and more times than not finish up fluffing or skinning the shot?

An almost foolproof way of getting the ball onto the green is to use a putter – yes, that's right, a putter! This is how it's done:

The address position is the same as if you are playing a short chip. The stance is open, the weight is concentrated on the left leg, and the hands are positioned ahead of the ball.

The secret of success is a soft wrist cock at takeaway so you can hit down on the ball, squeezing it between the head of the putter and the ground so that it pops up and out of the grass. Make sure you keep your hands ahead of the ball throughout.

Incidentally, the ball will pop onto the green with lots of roll, so allow for this by not hitting too hard at impact.

FROM THE FRINGE

Change the club – not your swing

Many golfers like to play all their short chip shots with a 'favourite' club. But some teachers think this is a mistake – because you need to change your swing for various distances, making a difficult part of the game even harder. It is much easier to repeat the same swing for all greenside chips. Let the loft of the various irons simply carry the ball on to the front of the putting surface and then roll it to the pin. A little time spent hitting same-weight shots will soon establish how far each club lofts the ball through the air and the amount of roll it generates. Remember, also, that it's much easier to judge roll than high loft and the spin it creates.

Around the green

DISTANCE CONTROL

Information at your finger tips

Although most golfers know roughly how far they hit each of their irons, very few are certain of the exact yardages they carry the ball with part-shots into greens with their lofted clubs.

One way to solve the problem is to hit enough balls with each lofted club to ascertain the distances of half, three-quarter and full shots.

Once satisfied that the yardages are correct, write them in order on a small piece of paper and stick it just below the grip so that you can read it when you need to carry a particular distance.

It's a good idea to cover the list with clear adhesive tape to protect it from the weather and damage from the club being continuously removed and returned in the bag.

Most players who use this system soon learn off-by-heart the various distances and then remove the chart.

55 yds.

80 yds.

100 yds.

½ 55 yds.
¾ 80 yds.
FULL 100 yds.

½ 55 yds.
¾ 80 yds.
FULL 100 yds.

SHORT GAME

Putt it there safely

The safest and often most effective way of getting the ball close to the pin from just off the green is with the chip-putt shot.

Although the flip-up lob from a few yards looks impressive to youngsters, it is a shot fraught with danger for all but good players, often resulting in an embarrassing 'thin' through the green.

All you have to do to get a good result is make sure your hands are ahead of the ball at address and then, with your normal putting action, stroke the ball to the target, ensuring there is no breaking of the wrists.

Placing a club shaft under the arms and across the chest helps underline that the necessary motion is an up-and-down pendulum action of the shoulders rather than a turn.

89

Around the green

THE HIGH LOB
Handy checkpoint

The high lob shot seems to cause real headaches to many high and mid-handicap players, particularly when it has to be played over trouble (like water or bunkers).

Anxiety and tension are the main causes of failure, with negative thoughts creeping in of duffing the ball into the trouble or thinning it through the green.

The best way to combat the problem is to have one simple thought in your mind when playing the shot – and an excellent one for the high lob is to make sure the back of the left hand and the clubface point to the sky at the end of the swing.

As far as the set-up is concerned, aim your feet, hips and shoulders a little left of the target but the leading edge of the club straight at it. Position the ball forward in your stance so that the hands are level or just behind it, and let your weight slightly favour the back foot.

THE FLAG

In or out?

Whether the flag is left in or taken out when the ball is in the fringe and just off the green can have an effect on your score.

Most top players and coaches agree that the pin is better left in when you are facing a slippery downhill putt because the flagstick makes the hole easier to see and the stick can act as a valuable 'brake' if you happen to strike the ball too hard.

If the shot is uphill and you can clearly see the hole, you can afford to be more aggressive and take the flag out.

Around the green

GREENSIDE CHIPS

Brush away those chipping problems

Are you one of the many golfers who have problems playing the simple chip shot from just off the green?

If the answer is 'yes' then it's a fairly safe bet that you've got the ball too far forward in your set-up – because to most people that's where it feels the most comfortable. The trouble is, however, that this position either causes the clubhead to strike the ball on the up (causing a 'thin') or to hit the turf before the ball.

You can find the right position by standing to the side of the ball and making a few practice swings, carefully noting where the clubhead first comes into contact with the ground.

That, quite simply, is exactly where the ball should be positioned in your stance.

PITCH SHOTS
It's not all about pin-point accuracy

A club pro I know often tells new pupils about two very good players who were locked in matchplay and faced with virtually identical 70-yard pitch shots into the final green. The match was all-square.

The first fired his ball as straight as an arrow and it flew directly over the pin before sitting down safely on the green and about five yards from the hole. He was well pleased and confidently stroked the putt to within inches of the cup for a conceded par.

The other player got it slightly wrong coming into the ball and pulled it to the left. It just managed to stay on the putting surface pin-high and about five yards from the hole. The player thudded his club into the ground in anger and frustration and was still breathing fire as he gripped his putter with the same pressure needed to strangle a poisonous snake. He gave line and length only cursory consideration before angrily striking the ball well past the hole. He missed the putt back – game lost.

Moral of the story: When it comes to the short game, distance is just as important as accuracy. Both pitch shots finished the same number of yards from the hole – so the one that flew straight over the pin was, in effect, no better than the other. There was no need for 'Mr Angry' to lose his temper..and, in doing so, the match.

Around the green PRACTICE TIPS

AROUND THE GREEN
Keep it simple

Complicated thoughts cause high handicappers all sorts of problems when it comes to the relatively simple task of chipping from just off the green.

The most common fault is, of course, the breakdown and flicking of the wrists through impact, closely followed by how far back and through you should take the club. Most poor greenside players make the mistake on short chips of taking the club too far back and then, to compensate, commit the cardinal sin of decelerating the clubhead through impact, causing thins and other erratic shots.

The easiest method to counter this is to concentrate on keeping the lengths of the backswing and followthrough exactly the same – short for short chips and getting progressively longer the further you get from the pin. A good practice drill to achieve equal-length swings is to stick tee pegs on the target line behind and in front of the ball and swing the club to them.

TEE TO GREEN

AROUND THE GREEN

Develop 'feel' for chips

A good way to develop feel on those delicate chip shots round the green is to grip well down the handle on a lofted club – the pitching wedge is as good as any – and hit balls using only your right hand.

Set up with the ball well back in your stance so that your hand is well ahead of it. Then, using a pendulum action similar to that of a long putt, allow the natural loft of the club to lift the ball off the turf and onto the green.

Practice until you can 'feel' the shot and then add your left hand to further increase control. You should soon see a big improvement.

Around the green — PRACTICE TIPS

AROUND THE GREEN

Get real when chipping

How many times have you emptied a tube of balls by the side of a practice green and, after a couple of 'feelers', chipped nearly all of them dead to the hole...only to find that out on the course your silky smooth action and accuracy have deserted you?

The reason is because, by hitting all your practice shots from the same spot, you have eliminated the 'one-chance-only' pressure factor from the situation.

Some teachers recommend that, in order to introduce reality and pressure, chipping practice should be carried out using one ball only and each chip should be followed up with a putt to get the ball into the hole.

If you think this is a bit extreme, spread your practice balls out so that each shot demands a different length of swing and approach path to the pin.

96

GREENSIDE CHIPPING
Well worth a pint!

After a few rounds where my greenside chipping was, to say the least, fairly unimpressive, I went to the practice area to try and sort things out... and became thoroughly bored with the whole thing within 10 minutes. As my mind just began conjuring up images of beer and the warm clubhouse bar, a chap I know appeared with a couple of clubs and a tube of balls under his arm and threw out a challenge for a chipping competition, with the loser picking up the tab for a couple of pints.

We each agreed to hit one ball from a number of spots round the green, the nearer the pin scoring a point and the first one to notch up 50 points being the outright victor. Half-an-hour later and we were still locked in battle, with my concentration firing on all cylinders and my chipping improved.

I thoroughly recommend introducing a competitive element to your short-game practice if you want to make it more meaningful and less boring.

PS – I picked up the tab!

Around the green PRACTICE TIPS

AROUND THE GREEN The breaking down of the wrists through impact – in other words, flicking at the ball – is one of the cardinal sins when it comes to playing chip shots. Here are a few simple remedies designed to help solve the problem. We guarantee at least one of them will work for you.

● **Focus on the handle**
After setting up to play the shot, look at the ball and think only of the handle of the club – taking it back and then moving it through and beyond impact.

● **Painful lesson**
Extend the length of your chipping club by gripping it together with another one. Only by using the correct action will you avoid giving yourself a nasty slap in the side every time you play the ball.

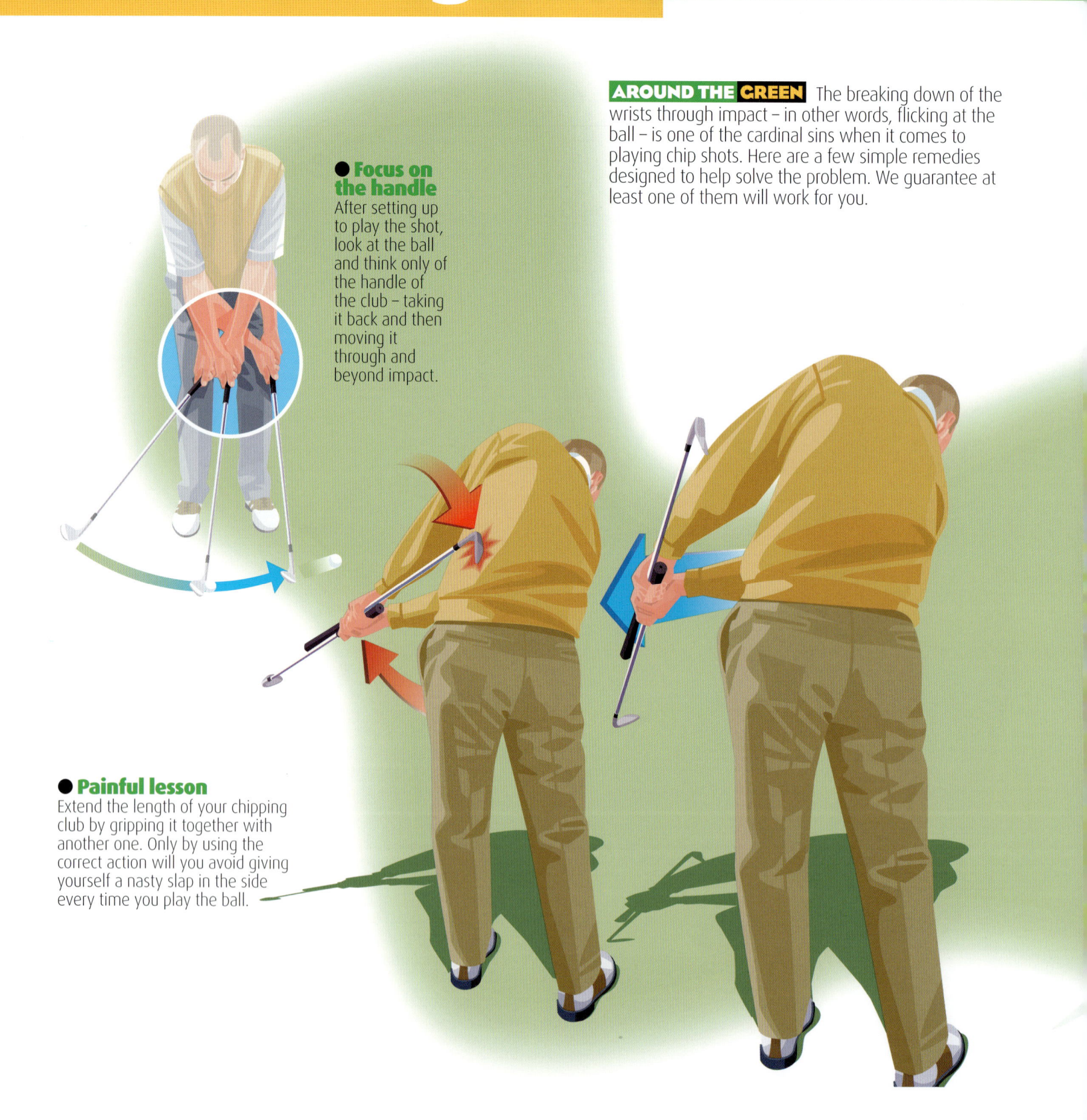

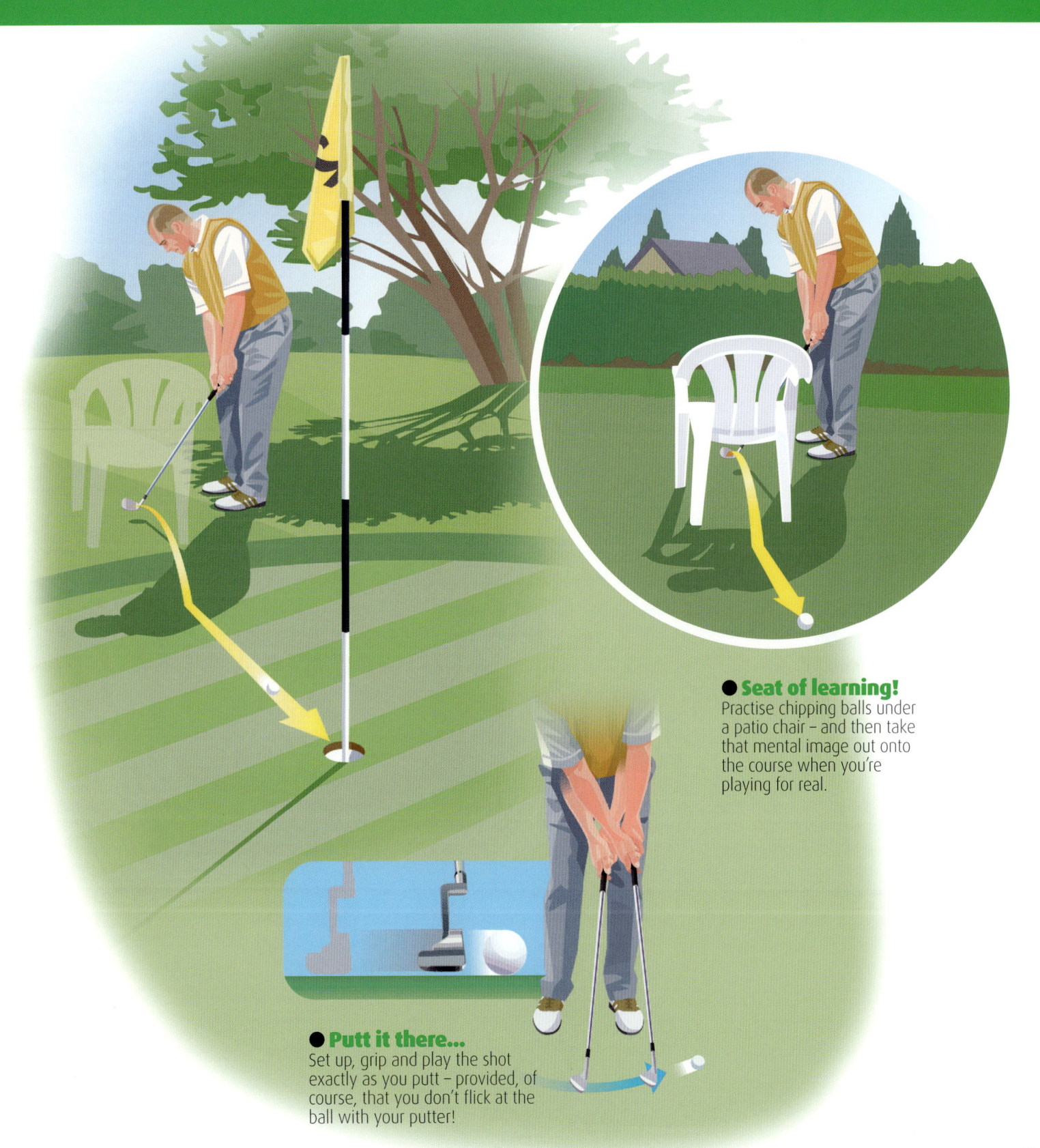

● **Seat of learning!**
Practise chipping balls under a patio chair – and then take that mental image out onto the course when you're playing for real.

● **Putt it there...**
Set up, grip and play the shot exactly as you putt – provided, of course, that you don't flick at the ball with your putter!

99

Around the green PRACTICE TIPS

After mastering one of the steps...

...go on to another.

AROUND THE GREEN
Steps to lower scores

Here's a simple indoors drill to help improve your greenside skills with a lofted club. But don't tell 'her indoors' we suggested it or she'll be after you for a new carpet!

Using your wedge or sand iron, stand at the bottom of your stairs and pick a step to pitch the ball onto.

Once you can get it to land and remain on that step regularly, select another one – higher or lower – and repeat the exercise.

In no time at all you should develop good feel for the weight of those awkward little shots that mean the difference between a good score and a bad one.

AROUND THE GREEN
Give your chips a lift

That old step ladder leaning against the shed can come in handy when you're brushing up your short game in the back garden.

A good drill, with the ladder upright, is to start by chipping balls over the first rung and gradually work your way up to the top, beginning with the less-lofted clubs and on through to the wedges.

To make it that much harder, low handicappers should use three balls and not proceed to the next step until all three have consecutively been 'potted' through the target gap.

Once you've scaled the dizzy heights to the top, lie the ladder on the ground and use the rungs to work on your distance control.

Around the green — PRACTICE TIPS

WITHIN 80 YARDS

Have a ball

It's surprising how many players make a complete hash of playing pitch shots from within 80 yards of the pin...the distance from which good scores are often put together.

One of the most common mistakes is the breakdown of the relationship formed by the arms and body at address. Instead of the arms following the upper body to the maximum point of the backswing – whether it be a full swing or only a part – and then back through to impact, they break away and the two fall out of 'sync'. All sorts of problems then occur, leading to a loss of accuracy, distance control and, very often, both.

You can check your action is correct by going onto the practice ground and lodging a soccer ball between your arms and chest at address. Any breakdown between the two will lead to the ball dropping or being squeezed out of the arms.

Once you have everything working together, it's a good idea to retain the ball image when called upon to play the shot for real.

CHIPPING ALIGNMENT

Square up for solid chips

Look at a poor chipper and you'll often discover they're making the all-too-common error of setting their shoulders open to the target line (pointing left of the flag).

Although the toes can be aligned slightly to the left, the shoulders are best kept square. Setting them left will encourage you to swing across the body from out-to-in, generally forcing the clubface to cut across the ball and make a glancing rather than solid contact.

Setting the shoulders square also helps to keep the hands ahead of the ball at address. Your job is then to make sure they stay ahead during the shot.

103

Around the green — PRACTICE TIPS

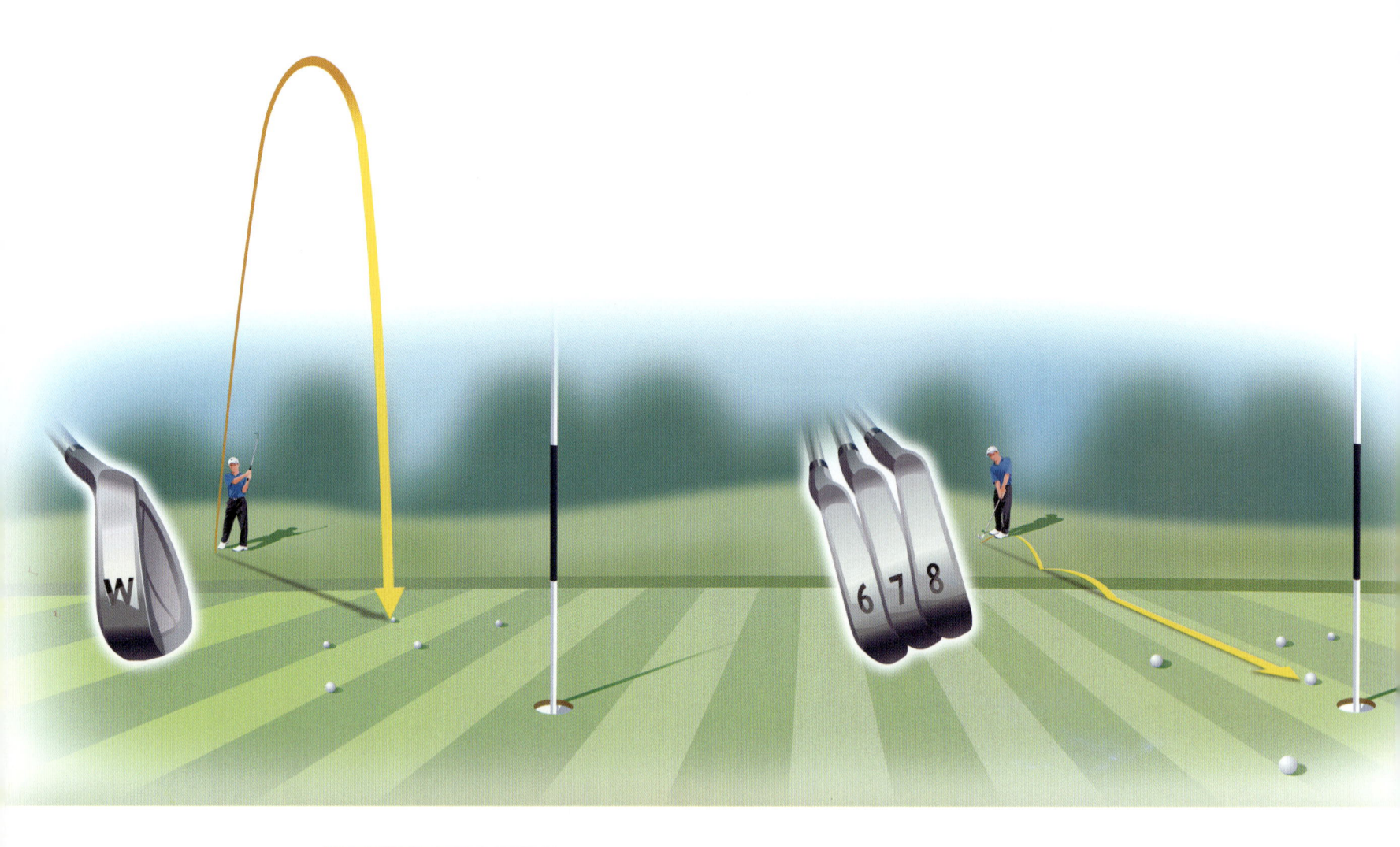

GREENSIDE CHIPS

Proving the point

Enjoying a pint in our clubhouse the other evening, I looked out to the par-3 18th hole and saw one of our promising youngsters had narrowly missed the green and was about to play to the hole.

I fully expected him to lob the ball high into the air and try to stop it quickly near the pin, à la Phil Mickelson. But he didn't.

Instead, he took a mid-iron from his bag and ran the ball low to the hole, giving him a fairly short putt for his par.

Mentioning my surprise to the club pro, he told me that he encourages the juniors to carry out their own test on the practice ground. "I get them to play 10 or 12 balls with a lofted wedge and the same number with a 6, 7 or 8-iron. Up to now, all but one has gone away convinced that the low route is by far the best bet," he said.

104

SHORT GAME
Make it real

I remember several years ago somehow managing to reach the semi-finals of a club knockout competition despite being a poor chipper from around the green.

So for a few days before the game I set aside half-an-hour each evening to put things right. By the time the big day arrived I was able to bunch a dozen or so balls quite tightly round the pin on the practice green.

But, as you've probably guessed, it all went horribly to pieces again soon after the match began and my opponent had a rather easy passage into the final.

The professional at the club soon told me what had gone wrong. "You have to try and create real playing conditions when you're practising pressure shots. By chipping a pile of balls one after another towards the pin, you removed the pressure and created an artificial situation," he explained.

He recommended that in future I used only one ball for this type of short-game practice – chipping it to the hole and then trying to sink it with the putter.

I suggest you try it…and discover just how good you really are!

On the green

Many prefer the conventional putter for long distances.

The broom-handle comes into its own near the hole.

ON THE GREEN
Long and short of it

There's nothing new to the theory of carrying two putters in your bag – a heavy one for slow greens and a light one for when they are running fast.

The same can be applied to broom-handle and conventional putters.

Although many players acknowledge the fact that the broom-handle is a great tool near the hole and virtually eliminates the all-too-common fault of flicking the wrists and pulling the ball to the left, few seem to get on well with it on long putts, finding it unwieldy.

Provided you do not break the rule of having a maximum of 14 clubs in your bag, the simple answer is to carry both.

ON THE GREEN
Get the perfect putter

Arms hang naturally from shoulders.

Poor posture.

Eyes above ball. Face parallel to ground.

Eyes well inside ball. Face not parallel.

There is an angle between arms and shaft.

The toe of the putter is raised.

The left forearm and shaft form straight line. The left wrist is arched.

Although most players appreciate the advantages of a simple pendulum action when putting, few realise that it is hard to achieve unless the length of the putter is correct. In fact, the vast majority of golfers use putters that are too long.

The correct length will naturally encourage the correct posture by tilting forward from the waist and the hips so your eyes are directly over the ball and your arms hang vertically down. Your face will feel as though it is perfectly parallel to the ground and the left forearm and shaft of the club form virtually a straight line.

From here, a natural pendulum action can be achieved, allowing the arms and putter to swing straight back and through along the target line.

A putter that is too long makes correct alignment almost impossible. The path of stroke becomes too much of an arc as the shoulders turn rather than slightly tilt. The overall stroke becomes too wristy, with the clubhead usually overtaking the hands and causing poor contact and roll.

On the green

ON THE GREEN

Look for the 'pro side'

One of the major differences between good and bad players is their attention to detail. And nowhere is it more evident than on the putting green.

As well as carefully examining the surfaces for pace, all good players make absolutely sure they are aware of any slopes and borrows before stepping up to play the ball.

That's why, if they do miss, they always do so on the high side of the hole, also commonly known as the 'pro' side.

A ball approaching from the high side has three chances of meeting up with the bottom of the cup – from the side, toppling in from just above, or catching the back of the hole and curling in.

It's got no chance from low side. And yet many of us still hit it there because we can't be bothered to do our homework.

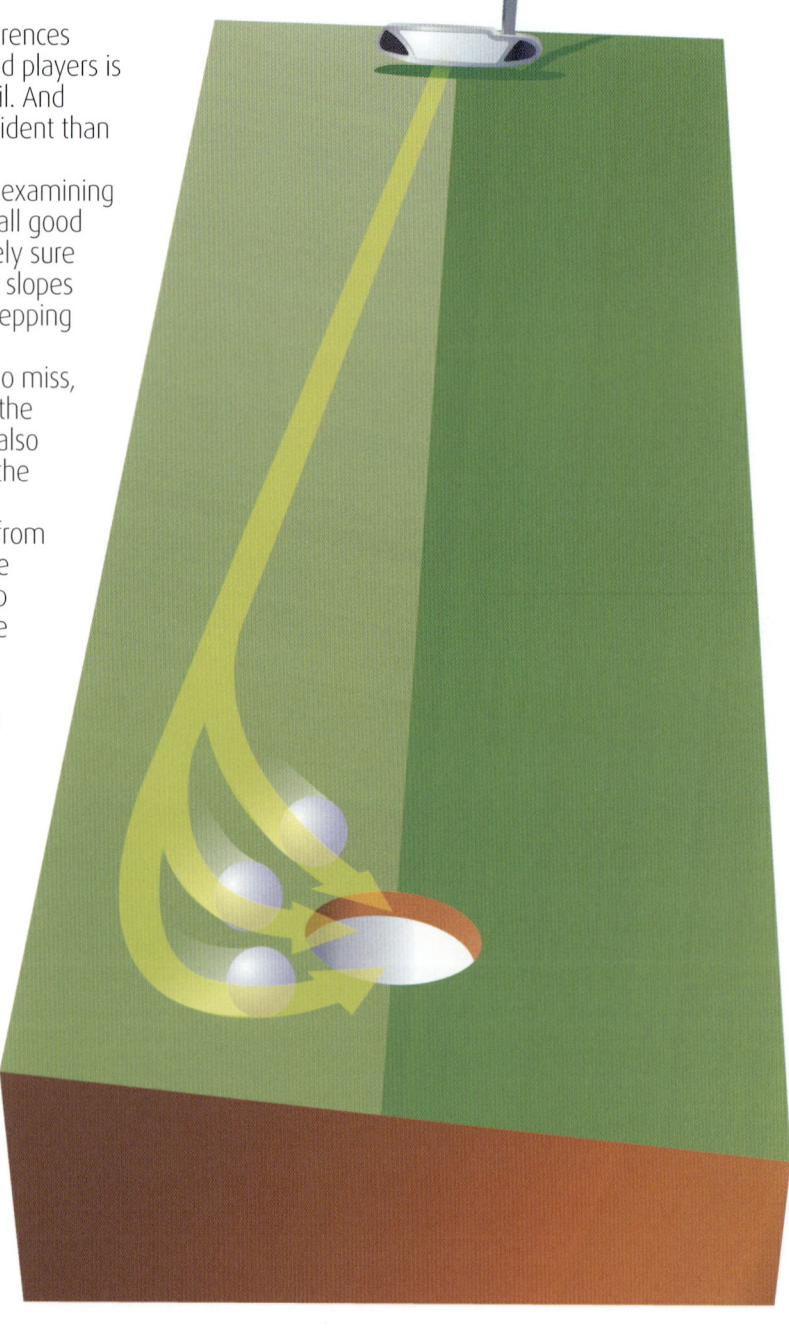

ON THE GREEN
Spin it to the hole

If you are having difficulty getting the ball up to the hole on medium and long range putts, check that you don't have it too far back in your stance.

If so, the hands will get ahead at address and lead to a downward strike on the ball – producing backspin and causing it to pull up short of the target.

If the ball is positioned further forward, with the hands above or even slightly behind the ball, the putter will strike the ball on the upswing, imparting topspin and causing it to roll further.

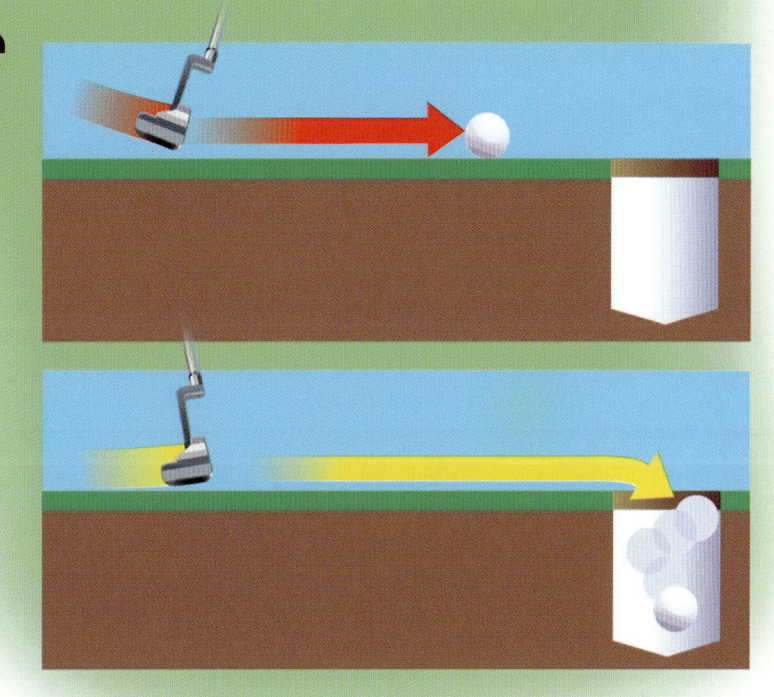

On the green

LONG PUTTS

Solid approach to long putts

Faced with long putts, the majority of mid and high handicappers commit the big mistake of concentrating on the length of their backswing rather than achieving a good and solid contact between the face of the putter and the ball.

Having taken a longer backswing than necessary, they then automatically decelerate the club through impact – causing a poor contact and the ball to pull up well short of the hole.

A good way to ensure the desired solid and accelerating stroke is to make a shortish backswing by simply rocking the shoulders and then allow both wrists to hinge slightly to move the head of the putter behind the hands and create more leverage and power.

Hold the hinge as the shoulders rock towards the target on the forward stroke and then let the head of the putter accelerate through the ball. Make sure the back of the left wrist faces the target through and beyond impact.

PUTTER ALIGNMENT
Get on the right line

A test carried out with a number of Tour professionals revealed, surprisingly, that over half of them failed to aim the faces of their putters within a one inch margin either side of the hole. So you can imagine the proportion of amateurs who are well wide of the target!

The best and most simple method to make sure the head is aimed correctly is to crouch down and, looking down the line of the putt, make sure it's square with the hole.

Be very careful not to move or twist the head of the club when you stand up and take up your address position.

And, talking of heads, remember one of the cardinal rules of putting and keep yours absolutely still when making the stroke.

On the green

PACE CONTROL

Read the lines to judge the speed

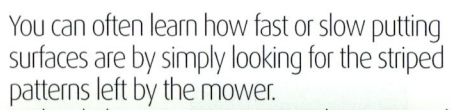

You can often learn how fast or slow putting surfaces are by simply looking for the striped patterns left by the mower.

The darker strip is cut against the grain and the lighter strip with it, meaning the darker grass will be standing more upright and will therefore provide more resistance to the ball. The lighter strip will be far slicker.

As far as reading whether your putt is uphill or downhill, remember to look carefully at the surrounding land. Greens tend to follow the general terrain.

TAKING AIM
Don't twist again

Look carefully at players who putt well and you will notice that they all take a lot of care and follow a set routine when they set themselves up for the stroke.

What most share in common is that they aim the face of the putter at the hole and then build their grip and stance around it, making sure not to alter the club's position.

Poor putters, on the other hand, grip the club, take up a stance and then twist their arms and body until they think they are on line. The usual result is a poor contact and the ball pushed to the right or pulled left.

On the green

READING THE LINE

'Defrost' your stroke

Make sure you don't over-complicate the relatively simple task of putting.

Too many amateurs stare at the line so long they begin to 'see' problems that just don't exist. By the time it comes to hitting the ball, they are filled with indecision and freeze – incapable of making a nice smooth stroke.

It's much better to take a quick look at the line from the back of the ball and beyond the hole, walk to your ball, take a brief look at the line you've selected and then concentrate on putting a good roll on the ball.

Although you won't necessarily sink more putts, you will certainly eliminate tension from your game...and prove more popular with those playing behind you!

Make sure you study the line of the putt...

...but don't spend too much time over it and run the risk of 'freezing'.

SHORT PUTTS

So easy to miss

The problem with putts of three feet and less are that they are too easy…to miss!

Youngsters (and, come to that, many adults) all too often take a quick look, amble up to the ball and smack it towards the hole…then watch in disbelief as it slides wide of the hole.

The fact that the ball is near the cup does not mean the basic fundamentals of putting can be forgotten, particularly alignment. It is still vitally important to ensure you are standing perfectly square to the line and accelerate the head of the putter through the ball.

Just watch the top pros. They tackle a short putt with the same degree of preparation as for a difficult shot from the tee or into a green. That's why they so rarely miss and their scores are so good.

115

On the green — PRACTICE TIPS

PUTTING PRACTICE

Game for improvement

Playing a round about a fortnight ago with a couple of keen juniors at our club, I was particularly impressed with the improvement in their putting since I last went out with them.

When I asked them how they'd got so much better, one of the lads said the club professional had come up with a series of putting games the juniors could play against each other on the practice green to introduce a competitive edge and make their practice more interesting.

"We always try to play at least one of the games before we go out on the course – and both our handicaps have come down since Mark [the pro] suggested them," said the 14-year-old, who is now only one shot off reaching single-handicap status.

After the round they showed me one of the games. A club is placed an agreed distance away and the first to go has to putt his ball short and within 4ft of it. The next player then has to putt short and within four feet of his opponent's ball…and so it continues until someone wins or the nominated number of balls have all been used and a draw is agreed.

Anyone fancy a game?

THE GRIP

Change for the better?

A change in the way you grip the putter often works wonders if your touch suddenly and without warning disappears on the greens.

Bernhard Langer is a wonderful example of someone who has fought and defeated the putting demons over the years by continually experimenting with the way he grips the club and by adopting various techniques.

Here are three tried-and-tested alternatives to the conventional overlapping grip.

Grip the bottom of the handle with your left hand, and both the handle and the left forearm with your right.

Adopt a conventional putting grip, but extend both index fingers so they point down the shaft.

Grip the top of the shaft with your right hand and place the left hand immediately below it.

117

On the green — PRACTICE TIPS

ON THE GREEN
Putt by the book

The best way to improve your consistency on the greens is to work on perfecting a pendulum putting action.

And an excellent drill to develop this action is to place an A4 book between your elbows and take up your normal putting stance and grip.

Keeping it in place while you putt back and through ensures that your shoulders, arms and hands all work as one unit as well as promoting rhythm and smoothness – other essential ingredients.

PUTTING PRACTICE

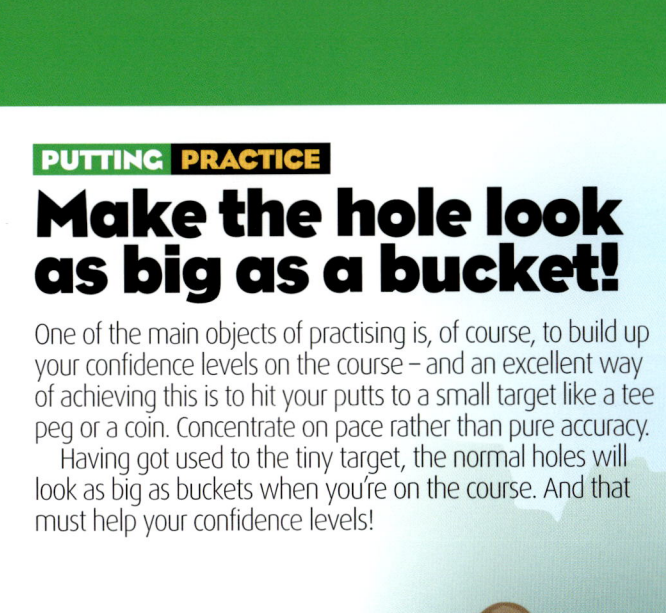

Make the hole look as big as a bucket!

One of the main objects of practising is, of course, to build up your confidence levels on the course – and an excellent way of achieving this is to hit your putts to a small target like a tee peg or a coin. Concentrate on pace rather than pure accuracy.

Having got used to the tiny target, the normal holes will look as big as buckets when you're on the course. And that must help your confidence levels!

119

On the green — PRACTICE TIPS

ON THE GREEN
Find your own tempo

Three golf balls and a flat surface at least 12 feet long can help you achieve one of the vital ingredients of good putting...consistency of tempo.

Hit a ball along the surface and then, without looking, try to putt the other two to the same spot as the first. Keep going until all three balls consistently pull up at the same spot.

Incidentally, everyone has their own individual tempo, which often reflects their pace of life. Study the tempo of the top players and you will soon spot that some are quicker than others. You have to establish your own tempo and then work on making it consistent.

PUTTING STROKE
Give leg movement the 'big boot'

One of the most common causes of missed putts is the movement of the legs during the stroke – so here's a very simple exercise to discover whether you're guilty and to help eliminate it.

Take up your normal stance and balance your putter against the right knee and thigh.

Place your right hand in front of your left and make your normal putting stroke. Movement of the club will indicate whether your legs are 'behaving themselves.'

It's sometimes useful to adopt a mental image of the drill when you are putting for real on the course.

In the bunker

OUT OF BUNKERS

Putt it there

Wet sand in the bunkers can make escape shots all the more difficult. Even low handicappers run the risk of their clubs either bouncing off the sand and into the middle of the ball (resulting in an embarrassing 'thin') or digging too deeply and robbing the clubhead of speed (usually leaving the ball in the bunker).

So before attempting the shot, closely examine the bunker. There could be an easier alternative.

Provided there is no lip to negotiate and the sand is fairly smooth and even, the putter can be used effectively to run the ball out of the bunker and onto the grass.

Simply adopt your normal putting stance and grip and concentrate on making a crisp and clean contact with the ball, ensuring the club is not grounded at address (breaking the rules) or does not strike any sand before reaching it.

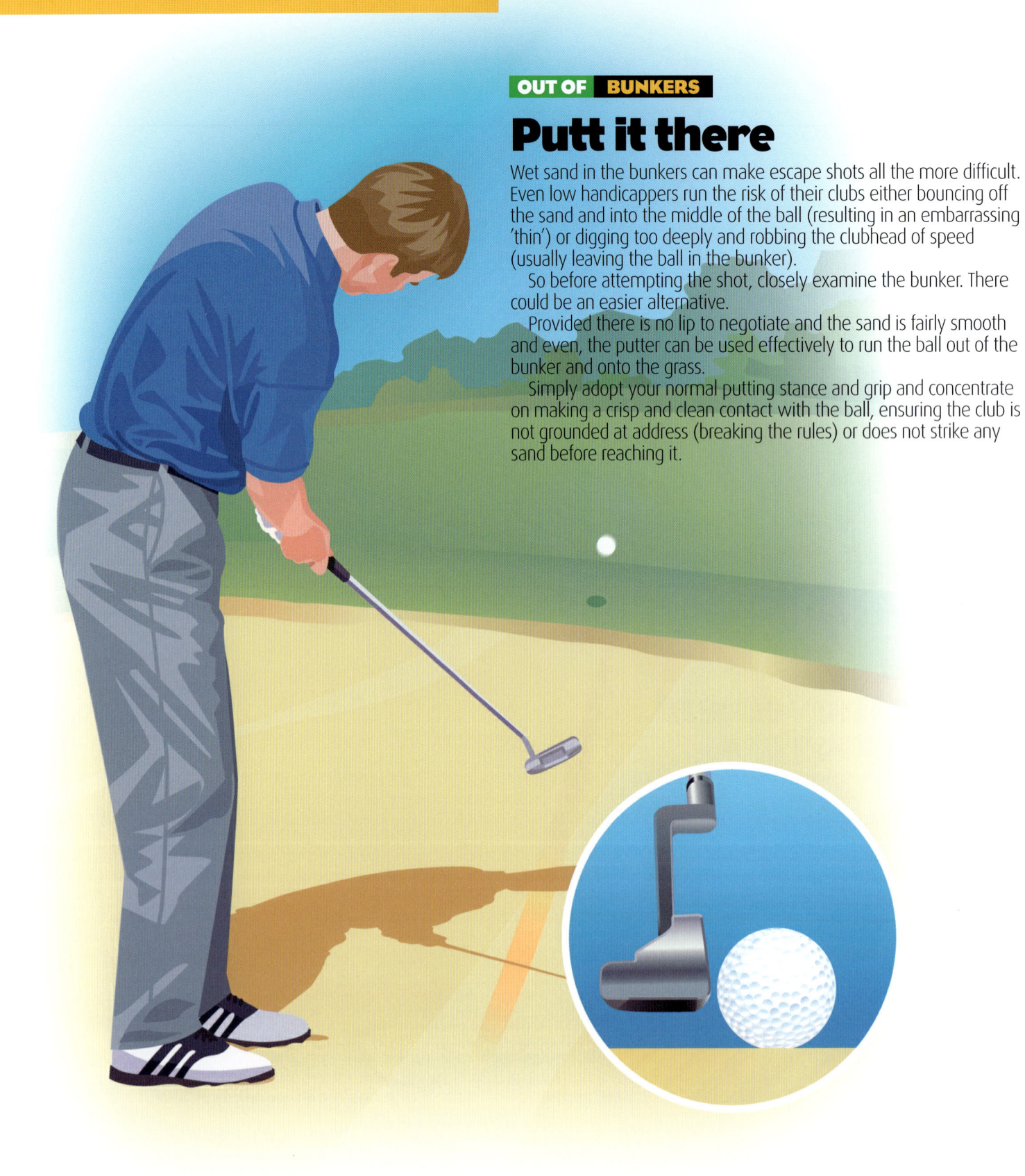

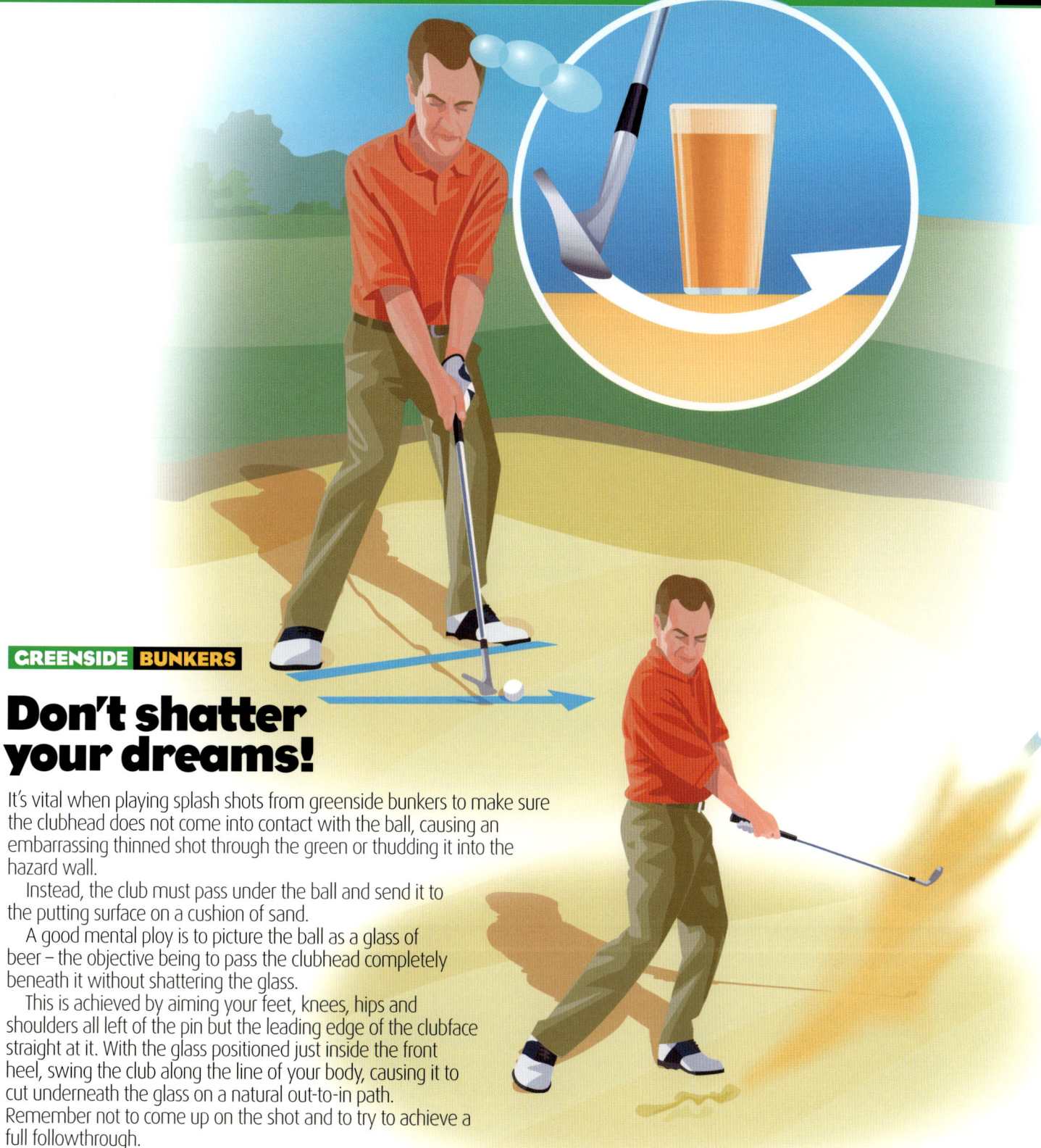

GREENSIDE BUNKERS

Don't shatter your dreams!

It's vital when playing splash shots from greenside bunkers to make sure the clubhead does not come into contact with the ball, causing an embarrassing thinned shot through the green or thudding it into the hazard wall.

Instead, the club must pass under the ball and send it to the putting surface on a cushion of sand.

A good mental ploy is to picture the ball as a glass of beer – the objective being to pass the clubhead completely beneath it without shattering the glass.

This is achieved by aiming your feet, knees, hips and shoulders all left of the pin but the leading edge of the clubface straight at it. With the glass positioned just inside the front heel, swing the club along the line of your body, causing it to cut underneath the glass on a natural out-to-in path. Remember not to come up on the shot and to try to achieve a full followthrough.

TEE TO GREEN

In the bunker

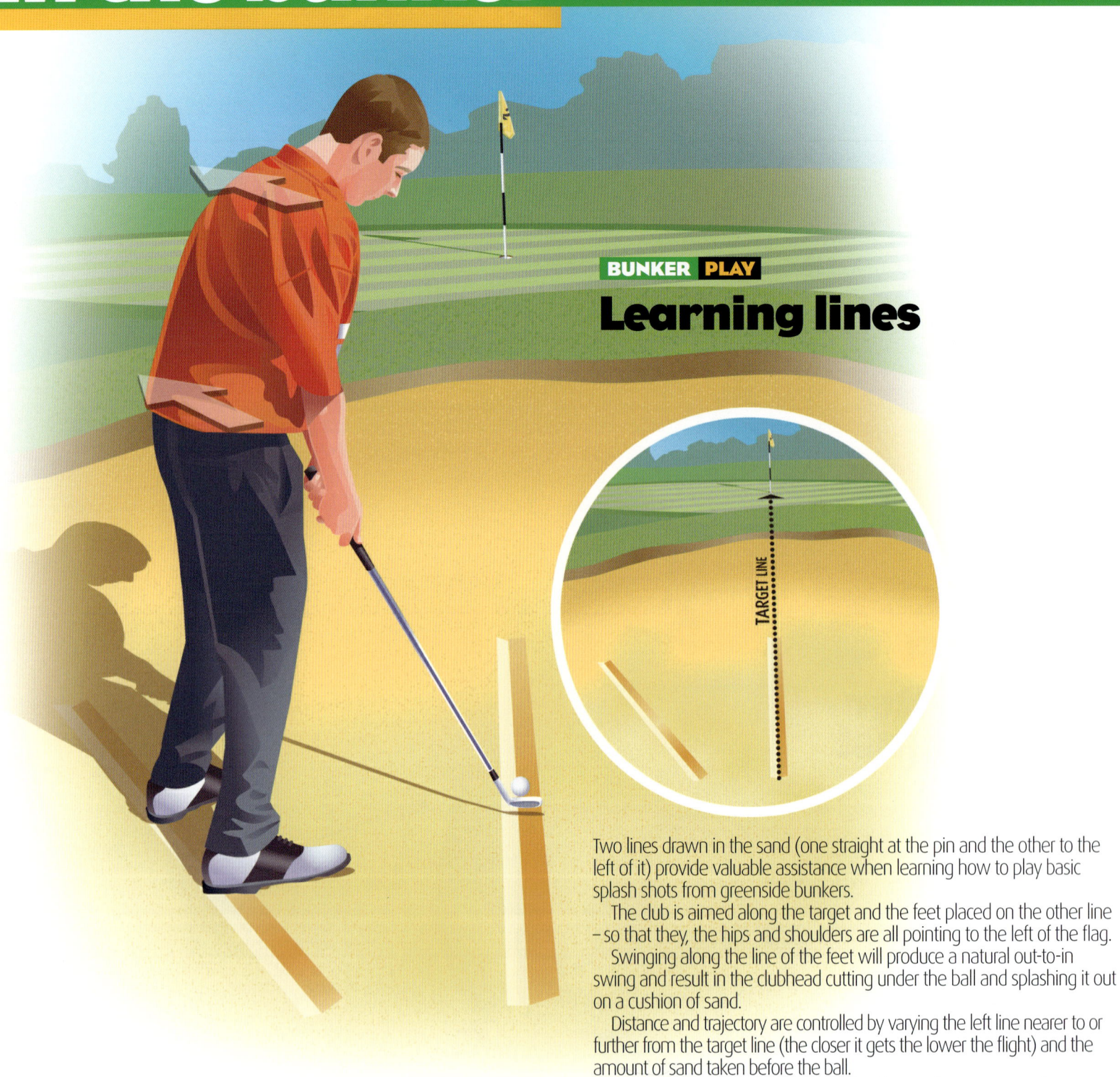

BUNKER PLAY
Learning lines

Two lines drawn in the sand (one straight at the pin and the other to the left of it) provide valuable assistance when learning how to play basic splash shots from greenside bunkers.

The club is aimed along the target and the feet placed on the other line – so that they, the hips and shoulders are all pointing to the left of the flag.

Swinging along the line of the feet will produce a natural out-to-in swing and result in the clubhead cutting under the ball and splashing it out on a cushion of sand.

Distance and trajectory are controlled by varying the left line nearer to or further from the target line (the closer it gets the lower the flight) and the amount of sand taken before the ball.

Incidentally, remember that the rules do not allow you to make any marks in the sand when you are playing competitive golf.

BUNKER PLAY
Finish on a high note

Although most mid and high handicap players, male and female, know the fundamental principles of greenside bunker play, very few of them master the splash shot.

One of the main reasons seems to be that, having set themselves up correctly for the shot, they then chop down into the sand and finish with the clubhead still firmly embedded.

Success largely depends on accelerating the clubhead down into the sand and under and through the ball TO A HIGH FINISH. Concentrating on the finish alone will help most players conquer their fear of playing from bunkers.

In the bunker

IN BUNKERS Do your brains become scrambled when faced with bunker shots? Well, here are five sand shots you can expect to encounter during a round and two simple thoughts to adopt when playing them.

Greenside splash

1 Aim your feet, hips and shoulders all left of the pin but the leading edge of the blade straight at it.

2 Concentrate on flying the ball to the green on a cushion of sand. The further you want the ball to fly, the less sand you take.

Plugged lie

2 Achieve a high, full finish.

1 Ensure the leading edge of the clubface is square to the target line.

126

Fairway bunker ▶

1 Hit the ball – not the sand.

2 Do not bury your feet deeply. Standing on top of the sand will help avoid digging the clubhead into it.

Upslope and downslope ▶

1 Angle your body at address to reflect the slope.

2 Hit through and under the ball. Do not try to scoop it into the air.

127

Trouble shots

HAMPERED BACKSWING

Restrictive practice

One of the most difficult shots in golf is when your backswing is restricted by an overhanging branch.

It's a situation that often ends in an embarrassing air shot or a sickening thud as the clubhead embeds itself either into the top of the ball or into the ground either side of it.

Try hitting the shot without a conventional backswing. Just set the clubhead so it's well clear of the trouble, look down at the ball without moving your body, and then swing down and through.

It sounds pretty simple, but, like most things connected with the game, it needs plenty of practice to perfect.

128

Toes in to avoid a duffer

FAIRWAY BUNKER

Having to stand in a fairway bunker and hit the ball from a bank above the feet wins a place in anyone's list of 'nightmare' shots...and usually ends in disaster.

Most players concentrate on gripping down the club and then working out how far the ball will naturally fly from right to left. They allow the slope to push their weight back onto their heels and end up virtually toppling over and completely out of control when they strike the ball.

The secret of success with this shot lies in building a firm and correctly balanced stance. Concentrate on digging the toes deeply into the sand so that you are standing as level as you possibly can to retain good balance throughout the swing.

Careful thought at address will put you in with a good chance of getting the ball where you want it to go.

Grip down the club to compensate for the ball being above the feet.

Keep your legs nicely flexed throughout the shot.

Dig the toes into the sand to level your stance and build a firm base.

TEE TO GREEN

Trouble shots

TROUBLE SHOOTING

Smooth your way over nasty trouble

The most important thing to remember when facing a shot over trouble to a green, particularly if it's water, is to rid yourself of tension and stress before you start the club back.

And the way to do that is to know that you've got more than enough club for the job. Don't concern yourself with the yardage to the far bank of the lake or stream, only with picking a club that will fly the ball to the back of the green – irrespective of pin position.

Once that's settled, all you then have to do is take a few deep breaths and concentrate on keeping your swing silky smooth.

The final thing to remember is to resist the temptation to 'come off' the shot by moving up too soon. Keep looking down until the ball is flying high to the target.

IN THE ROUGH
Not such a lucky break

Most players think they're in luck when they hit into the rough and discover the ball sitting perched on a clump of grass. But it can spell disaster unless the shot is tackled correctly.

It's easy to believe that you've been blessed with the perfect lie and all that's required is to smash it out onto the fairway or green.

The chances are, however, that if you set up normally only the top half of the clubface will make contact with the ball, resulting in a serious loss of power and distance. Depending on the exact height of the ball, the clubhead can actually pass right under it with no contact at all.

The answer to the problem is to hover the clubhead above the ground at address so that its leading edge is level with the bottom of the ball. Then go ahead and make your normal swing, ensuring you retain the angle of the spine formed at address.

Trouble shots

SIMPLE THOUGHTS
Here we turn our attention to playing from the four most awkward grassy lies you can expect to encounter on the course.

A 7-iron will do the job of a 6 on a downhill slope.

● Downhill
On a downhill lie, allow for the fact that the slope will effectively rob the clubface of some of its loft – so reach for one club less than you would normally use for the distance (say a 7 instead of a 6). Stand at 90° to the incline so that the majority of your weight is on the lower foot, position the ball a little further back than normal to avoid the clubhead thudding into the ground, and swing smoothly down the slope.

Don't make the all-too-common error of trying to help the ball into the air with a scooping action of the wrists.

SMOOTH

132

● Ball below feet

The flight of the ball from this lie will automatically be left to right – so remember to allow for it when you take aim. Help get the clubhead down to the ball and avoid a thin or topped shot by holding the grip at the top end and flex and bend your knees a little more than normal. Concentrate on staying fully down through the hitting area.

Incidentally, if you have difficulty remembering the natural direction the ball will take, think of it as an aircraft flying off and away from the slope rather than into it.

Hold the grip at the top end.

Flex and bend the knees a little more than normal.

Flight path

Aim here

AWKWARD LIES CONTINUED OVER

133

Trouble shots

SLOPES MADE EASY Here are the two other sloping lies you can expect to encounter from time to time and some simple thoughts on how to cope with them successfully.

Swing smoothly through the ball and up the slope.

● Uphill
As with the downhill shot, let the shape of your set-up reflect the slope, with your weight naturally favouring the lower foot. The ball needs to be positioned slightly further forward than when you're on level ground, and its flight will be higher than normal (so allow for it when you select a club). Now simply go ahead and swing smoothly through the ball and up the slope.

The flight from an uphill lie will be higher than normal.

● **Ball above feet**

As the ball is closer to you than from a normal lie, grip well down the handle and flex your knees a little rather than bending them. The slope will lead to a flatter-than-normal swing and the ball will automatically move through the air from right to left (remember the aircraft!). Obviously, the more severe the slope, the more you need to aim to the right to compensate.

Grip down the handle.

Flex the knees a little – don't bend them.

Aim here

Flight path

Trouble shots

TROUBLE SHOTS Even the tour pros now and again find themselves in deep trouble on the course – so why should we expect the luxury of stress-free rounds? Here we look at five situations in which you could well find yourself and offer some simple points to remember to get you back on the right track.

● Against a tree
Select a lofted club, turn your back on the target and stand with the ball about six inches outside your right foot. Hold the club with your right hand only – it will naturally sit on the toe – and, keeping the arm fairly straight, make sure you accelerate the clubhead into and through the ball. Make sure you stay down on the shot.

● Deep rough
The need here is to get the clubhead steeply into the ball to avoid it becoming tangled in the thick grass. This is achieved by having the ball well back in the stance, your weight concentrated on the front foot, and hingeing the wrists early in the backswing. Although sometimes difficult to achieve, try to make a full followthrough after impact.

● In a divot
Select a club you know has ample loft to get the ball up and away. Then concentrate on driving the clubhead down into the back of the ball with the intention of taking another divot within the existing one. Do not attempt to help the ball into the air and remember that the nature of the shot will result in the followthrough being restricted.

● **Bare lie near green**
Because of its snag-free rounded sole, the lofted fairway wood is ideal for this awkward little test. Grip down the handle with your normal putting grip and then putt it onto the green with a wrist-free arms and shoulders swing.

● **Plugged lie in bunker**
Forget all about angles of bounce and splashing balls out on cushions of sand. This is a shot where you need to align your body and clubhead square to the target and then hit down sharply about two inches behind the ball. Set-up essentials are: ball in the centre of stance, feet wriggled into sand for a firm base, and weight mainly on front foot.

Fault fixing

SLICE AND HOOKS

Earthy solutions

Most of us simply fall apart when, during a round, we suddenly and without warning start slicing or hooking the ball (or both) all over the place.

Thoughts desperately and instinctively turn to such mind-numbing subjects as knuckles visible on left hand, alignment, ball position, path of the swing, clubface position at impact and, horror of horrors, swingplane. Then our game dives even further downhill.

Well here's a simple little check that could solve your problems at a glance...literally.

After hitting a bad 'un, examine the divot. If you've sliced, there's more than a sporting chance that it's from right to left, because the most common cause is an out-in-path by the clubhead through the ball. So just concentrate for the rest of the round on creating straight divots.

Those who hook are likely to find their divots are from left to right as the clubhead travels through the hitting zone on an in-to-out path. The cure is the same as for the slice.

138

THE SLICE

Give your slice the elbow

Examine the swing of a slicer and you are likely to find that the path of the clubhead through the impact zone is from out-to-in rather than the correct in-to-square-to-in. The former action causes the face of the club to cut across the ball and impart clockwise spin and give it a distance-robbing left-to-right flight through the air.

The root cause can often be traced to the movement of the right shoulder at the start of the downswing. Instead of dropping, it turns horizontally and the right arm moves well away from the body.

The most simple cure is to concentrate on tucking the right elbow into the side in the downswing. This will automatically drop the right shoulder and put the club on the correct path into and through the striking zone, resulting in more solid hits and greater consistency.

Fault fixing

WINDY CONDITIONS
Brush up your short game

Strong and gusty winds usually play havoc with your game and lead to dropped shots. But you can help avoid a complete scoring disaster by spending a little extra time brushing up your short game before starting a round. Low chip shots under the wind and a 'hot' putter will help you claw back potential lost shots when your ball is blown about and consistently comes to rest just off the greens.

ON THE COURSE
Widen your stance

The normal width of stance (heels at shoulder-width apart) can prove a little unstable when the wind is blowing...so it's a good idea to widen it to establish a more solid foundation for your swing.

But be careful not to overdo it and restrict an easy (and necessary) hip and body turn. Three or four extra inches between the heels is ample.

Improve the lie by all means...but not by too much.

PREFERRED LIES
Hard lesson to learn

One of the compensations of winter golf is the fact that the vast majority of clubs encourage players to protect fairways by playing improved lies. But be careful not to make the same mistake I made several years ago.

A really good spell of play (including reaching the final of my club's winter knockout tournament) filled me with confidence that my handicap would tumble in the spring.

But the 'big push forward' just didn't happen. In fact, my scores got worse and my handicap increased by a stroke after the first couple of medal rounds.

A friend spotted the problem. Sitting the ball up nice and high on the fairways during winter had left me believing that perfectly acceptable natural lies were now bad ones. My mental approach was all wrong.

After a few sessions on the practice ground hitting balls out of divots and other really poor lies, I returned to the course fully appreciating the real difference between good and bad ones.

I have made a point ever since of making sure I don't make things too easy on the course during winter...and going to the practice ground every so often specifically to hit shots from bad lies.

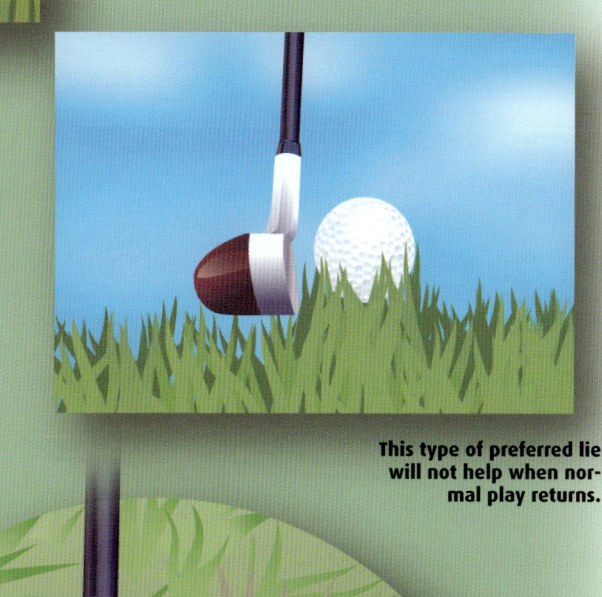

This type of preferred lie will not help when normal play returns.

Make sure you hit some shots off poor lies on the practice ground.

141

Fault fixing

TRAJECTORY CONTROL
Fix the ball flight with your eyes

HIGH TRAJECTORY

Take your normal set-up and look into the sky to the point where you want the ball to reach its maximum height. Holding that posture and returning your eyes to the ball will automatically lower your right shoulder, set most of your weight on your right side and encourage a shallow swingpath – exactly the things you need to hit a high shot successfully.

LOW TRAJECTORY

Look at a low spot along your intended ball flightpath to set your shoulders automatically nearly level and place more weight on your left side. The steeper-than-normal angle of attack will trap the ball at impact with a delofted clubface and send it off on a low flightpath.

Course management

COURSE TACTICS

Time to break a golden rule

During times of wet weather we can happily ignore one of the golden rules of chipping from just off the green – keeping the ball low to get it rolling with topspin as soon as possible on the putting surface.

Because the fringes are often very wet and the soft greens unpredictable as a result of spike marks and heel indentations, the most effective way to get the ball to stop near the pin is to send it in high with a lofted club, probably your sand or lob wedge.

Incidentally, remember to trust the natural loft on the clubface. Don't try to 'help' the ball into the air with a scooping action...it will almost certainly end in an embarrassing thinned shot through the green.

OFF THE TEE

Get a grip

One of essential ingredients of a solid swing is a firm foundation. But achieving one is almost impossible when teeing grounds become churned up and muddy. Remember, there is nothing in the rules that says you must tee your ball up in a direct line with the markers. And although you are definitely not allowed to tee the ball ahead of them, you can play from as far back as two clublengths. This will almost certainly allow you to find a firmer footing and more than compensate for the loss of the couple of yards or so! Also, remember to make sure before every full shot that the spikes in your shoes are free from grass and mud. A pitchmark repairer soon does the job.

TEE TO GREEN

Course management

FROM THE TEE

Play your favourites

Look carefully at par 5s and, unless you are a big hitter and can definitely reach the green in two, carefully plan a three-shot strategy using your favourite clubs. It will do your confidence (and the chance of a par) a power of good.

Say, for instance you're playing this 510-yarder.

The wood player could hit a driver (230 yards), followed by a 5-wood (210) to leave a 70-yard pitch to the flag.

An iron enthusiast, on the other hand, could play a 3-iron (190 yards) and a 4 (180) to leave a 140-yard approach with a 7 or 8.

So decide on YOUR strengths and weaknesses before automatically reaching for the 'big stick' on the tee.

FROM THE TEE
Set-up to stay dry

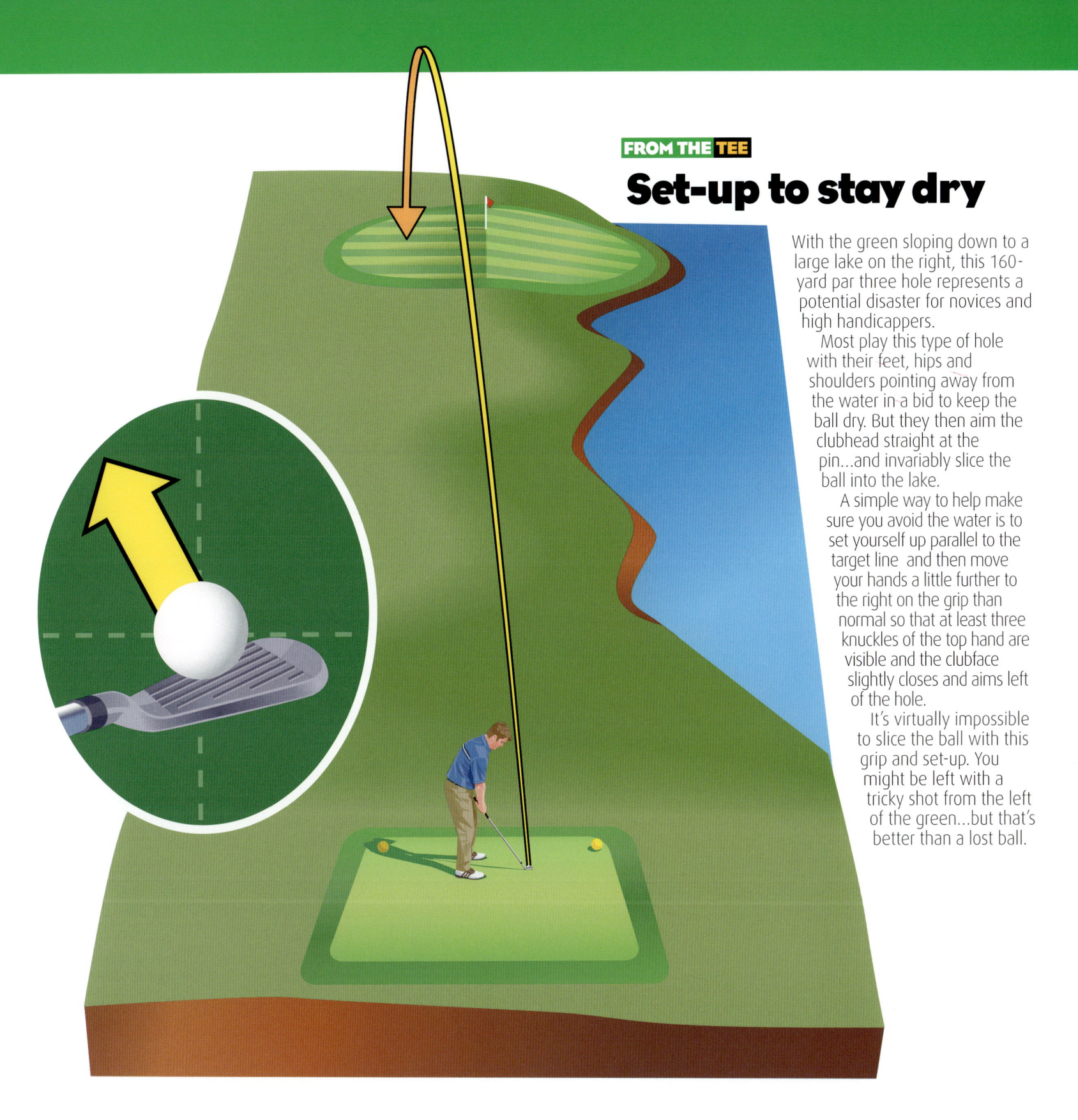

With the green sloping down to a large lake on the right, this 160-yard par three hole represents a potential disaster for novices and high handicappers.

Most play this type of hole with their feet, hips and shoulders pointing away from the water in a bid to keep the ball dry. But they then aim the clubhead straight at the pin...and invariably slice the ball into the lake.

A simple way to help make sure you avoid the water is to set yourself up parallel to the target line and then move your hands a little further to the right on the grip than normal so that at least three knuckles of the top hand are visible and the clubface slightly closes and aims left of the hole.

It's virtually impossible to slice the ball with this grip and set-up. You might be left with a tricky shot from the left of the green...but that's better than a lost ball.

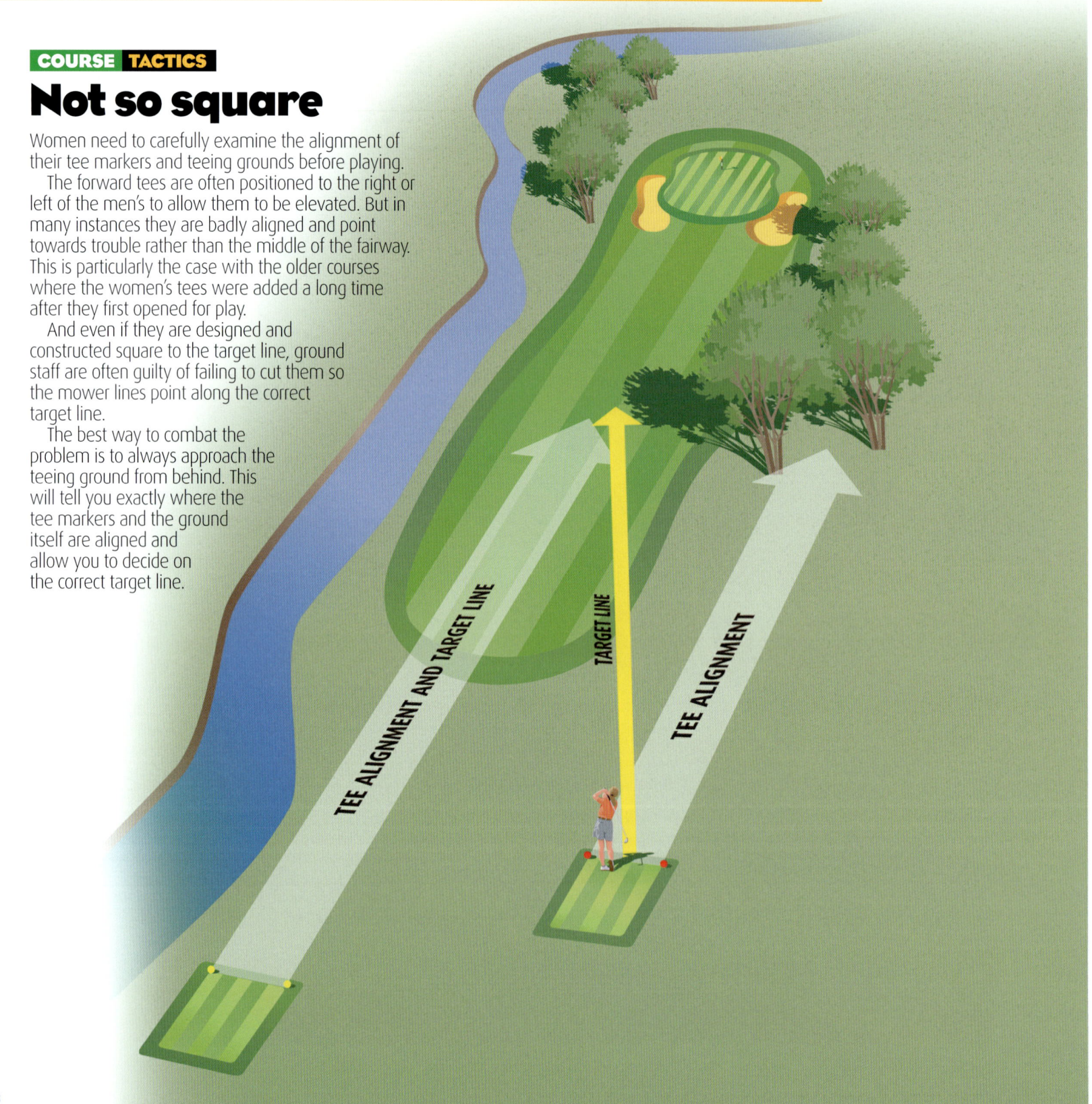

Course management

COURSE TACTICS

Not so square

Women need to carefully examine the alignment of their tee markers and teeing grounds before playing.

The forward tees are often positioned to the right or left of the men's to allow them to be elevated. But in many instances they are badly aligned and point towards trouble rather than the middle of the fairway. This is particularly the case with the older courses where the women's tees were added a long time after they first opened for play.

And even if they are designed and constructed square to the target line, ground staff are often guilty of failing to cut them so the mower lines point along the correct target line.

The best way to combat the problem is to always approach the teeing ground from behind. This will tell you exactly where the tee markers and the ground itself are aligned and allow you to decide on the correct target line.

GAME IMPROVEMENT

Make it easy on yourself

I remember several years ago being approached by a youngster on the 12th tee of my local club if he could join myself and my teenage son for the remaining six holes of our round. He said he had just started playing the game and had been unable to find anyone to play with or filter-in on the course that particular day.

He hit a nice little drive down the fairway and then, to my surprise, teed his ball up on a tuft of grass to play his second shot. His ball ran into the rough, where he again sat it up on top of the grass before playing it.

I thought it would be only right and helpful to point out to him that what he was doing was against the rules, to which he replied. "Yes, I know. But the pro has told me to learn to hit these easy shots before we go on to tackle the hard ones."

"That's fine – you must carry on doing what the pro recommends," I said, thinking what a great piece of advice to build up the lad's confidence and enjoyment of the game.

A few years later the youngster was the club scratch champion and had won a place in the county squad.

I'm sure much of his success was down to the wisdom of our club professional.

149

Course management

DISTANCE CONTROL

Starting with the wedge...

Although most players can accurately visualise how far they hit their pitching wedge, many have problems when it comes to judging longer distances (particularly on courses they are not familiar with).

A good way of solving the problem is to stand by your ball and imagine where your full pitching wedge will land. Then just add a visual 10 yards beyond that spot for a 9-iron, another 10 for an 8-iron and so on.

Incidentally, remember when playing into a green to judge the distance to the centre or back rather than the front. The vast majority of approach shots finish well short of the pin.

PRE-MATCH NERVES
Play YOUR game at all times

Many women do not enjoy playing in mixed competitions because they feel intimidated by the power and long hitting of some of their male partners or opponents.

There is, of course, no need for this. The forward positioning of the women's tees and the handicap system are there to compensate fully for any differences.

Before setting up to play a shot (whether it be from a tee, fairway or the rough), decide on a target you know you can hit and then concentrate on putting the ball there. Never try to hit the ball too hard or attempt to play a shot where your doubts outweigh your confidence.

151

Course management

COURSE MANAGEMENT

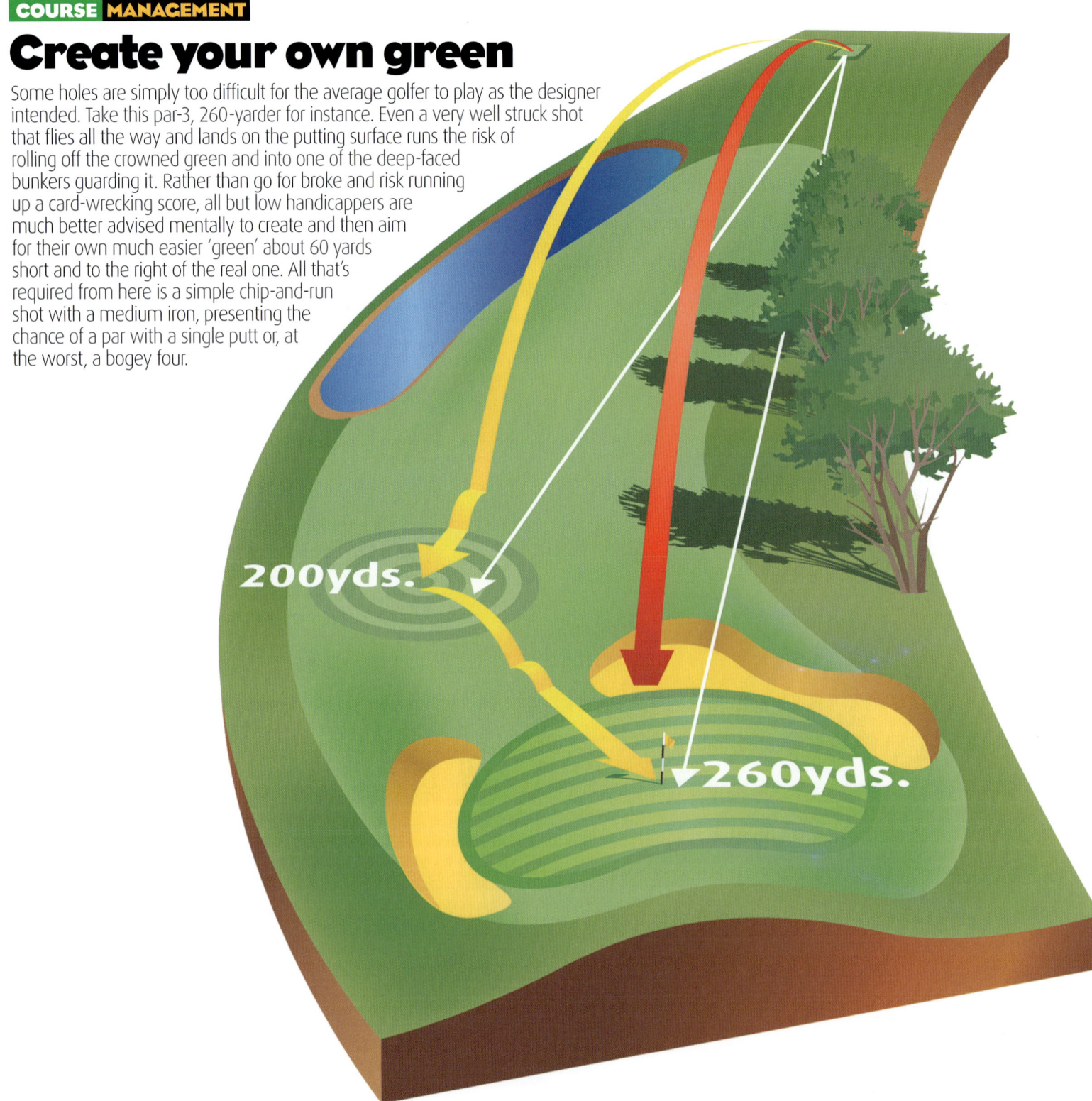

Create your own green

Some holes are simply too difficult for the average golfer to play as the designer intended. Take this par-3, 260-yarder for instance. Even a very well struck shot that flies all the way and lands on the putting surface runs the risk of rolling off the crowned green and into one of the deep-faced bunkers guarding it. Rather than go for broke and risk running up a card-wrecking score, all but low handicappers are much better advised mentally to create and then aim for their own much easier 'green' about 60 yards short and to the right of the real one. All that's required from here is a simple chip-and-run shot with a medium iron, presenting the chance of a par with a single putt or, at the worst, a bogey four.

200yds.

260yds.

COURSE TACTICS

Time to drop the driver?

The reason most players hit the ball further with their driver than with any other club is simply because, in addition to its length of shaft, its minimal loft creates a low trajectory to produce plenty of forward roll on landing. But through the air, there's hardly any difference between the 'big stick' and the 3-wood.

Which, when the fairways are wet and muddy – producing little or no roll on the ball – begs the question: why bother to include the driver in your bag?

Next time you're playing a casual round in these conditions, put the driver and 3-wood head-to-head.

You'll probably find the driver's normal distance advantage will disappear and the easier-to-use and more accurate 3-wood will run out the comfortable winner.

It's time to give the driver a well-earned rest until the sun shines and the run returns to the fairways.

A driver's lesser loft gives a low trajectory and more roll.

A 3-wood has extra loft which sends the ball higher. It can match a driver for distance through the air.

Course management

THINK ABOUT IT The difference between a good score and a bad one is often simply down to those few vital seconds before the tee shots...and whether you step up and just blast away at the ball or spend a few moments carefully thinking about how you should play the hole ahead. Here are three typical examples where a little thought about tactics can knock shots off your card.

● Focus on the positive

Wherever you look from the tee, there's trouble staring back at you on this short par 4 hole...trees along each side, a pond 130 yards out and huge bunkers guarding the green. Concentrating on avoiding the trouble will almost certainly lead to a nervous and quick lunge at the ball rather than a smooth and controlled swing. The secret of playing this tee shot is therefore to eliminate the negatives from your mind and find something positive at which to aim.

On this particular hole, there's a church spire directly behind the green. That is your target...so take care in aligning yourself and swing smoothly through the ball. Then watch it fly comfortably over the pond and onto the fairway to leave you a short pitch into the green.

154

● Big hits – big trouble

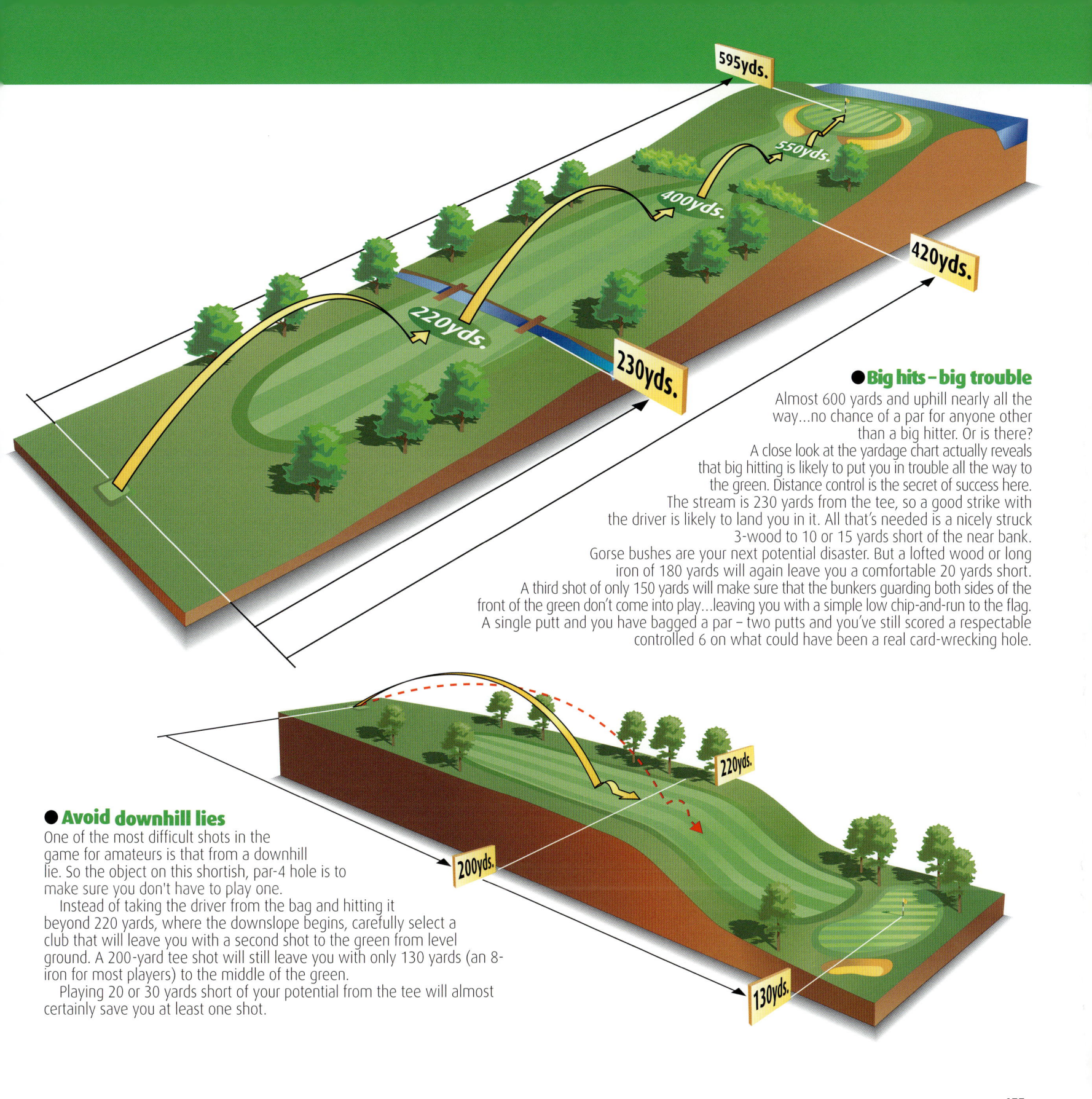

Almost 600 yards and uphill nearly all the way...no chance of a par for anyone other than a big hitter. Or is there?
A close look at the yardage chart actually reveals that big hitting is likely to put you in trouble all the way to the green. Distance control is the secret of success here. The stream is 230 yards from the tee, so a good strike with the driver is likely to land you in it. All that's needed is a nicely struck 3-wood to 10 or 15 yards short of the near bank.
Gorse bushes are your next potential disaster. But a lofted wood or long iron of 180 yards will again leave you a comfortable 20 yards short.
A third shot of only 150 yards will make sure that the bunkers guarding both sides of the front of the green don't come into play...leaving you with a simple low chip-and-run to the flag. A single putt and you have bagged a par – two putts and you've still scored a respectable controlled 6 on what could have been a real card-wrecking hole.

● Avoid downhill lies

One of the most difficult shots in the game for amateurs is that from a downhill lie. So the object on this shortish, par-4 hole is to make sure you don't have to play one.

Instead of taking the driver from the bag and hitting it beyond 220 yards, where the downslope begins, carefully select a club that will leave you with a second shot to the green from level ground. A 200-yard tee shot will still leave you with only 130 yards (an 8-iron for most players) to the middle of the green.

Playing 20 or 30 yards short of your potential from the tee will almost certainly save you at least one shot.

Course management

COURSE TACTICS

Look what's ahead…

It's surprising how many players make the game so much harder than it need be simply by not using common sense on some holes.

I remember playing a particular par 5 for the first time in the summer and, after hitting a perfectly reasonable drive, struck a good 5-wood to within about 80 yards of the green.

When I got to the ball I found it was on a really severe downhill slope…and thinned it into a small stream guarding the front of the green. I walked to the next tee writing a 7 on my card instead of a potential 4.

A close look at the course planner before I hit the second shot would have revealed that I'd have been much better off playing the ball to level ground about 30 or 40 yards further back to leave me a fairly simple 9-iron.

...and behind

It's also well worth carefully studying the course planner for contours and features *behind* the greens when you're playing par 4s and 5s for the first time.

Mounds can act as very useful 'backstops' if you happen to catch one a bit thin and should come into the reckoning when you're planning where you want to hit your drive (or second shot on a long par 5).

On the other hand, water or other nasty hazards behind a particular section of the green will pinpoint where you definitely *don't* want to be playing from.

Course management

TEE TACTICS

Through the hoop

There's a really useful piece of advice recommended by teaching guru Butch Harmon if you are on the tee and looking down a hole with plenty of trouble ahead.

Pick the safe area you want to reach and then imagine there's a hula hoop a few feet in front of you that you are going to hit the ball through. This concentrates your mind on the positive shot rather than the negative one into the trouble ahead.

It's also much easier mentally to hit the ball through the hoop than to a small target 200 yards or so away.